a fate worse than death

nisha patel

a fate worse than death

poems

ARSENAL PULP PRESS
VANCOUVER

ARSENAL PULP PRESS
Suite 202 – 211 East Georgia St.
Vancouver, BC V6A 1Z6
Canada
arsenalpulp.com

The publisher gratefully acknowledges the support of the Canada Council for the Arts and the British Columbia Arts Council for its publishing program and the Government of Canada and the Government of British Columbia (through the Book Publishing Tax Credit Program) for its publishing activities.

Arsenal Pulp Press acknowledges the xʷməθkʷəy̓əm (Musqueam), Sḵwx̱wú7mesh (Squamish), and səlilwətaɬ (Tsleil-Waututh) Nations, custodians of the traditional, ancestral, and unceded territories where our office is located. We pay respect to their histories, traditions, and continuous living cultures and commit to accountability, respectful relations, and friendship.

Cover art, illustrations, and text design by Nisha Patel
X-rays courtesy of Nisha Patel
Typesetting by Jazmin Welch
Edited by Natalie Wee
Copy-edited by Catharine Chen
Proofread by Alison Strobel

Printed and bound in Canada

Library and Archives Canada Cataloguing in Publication:
Title: A fate worse than death / Nisha Patel.
Names: Patel, Nisha, 1992– author.
Description: Poems.
Identifiers: Canadiana (print) 20230549918 | Canadiana (ebook) 20230549926 |
    ISBN 9781551529455 (softcover) | ISBN 9781551529462 (EPUB)
Subjects: LCGFT: Poetry.
Classification: LCC PS8631.A82945 F38 2024 | DDC C811/.6—dc23

contents

Part 2: disease

Part 2: disease

Part 3: disability

Author's Note

The materials and events in this book are real.

I started the excavation of what being disabled meant to me within my mouth. I asked for a copy of my dental X-rays while taking a research-creation class with Jordan Abel, confirming the extent of the cavities I'd let fester in periods of deep illness. Looking for proof ended up becoming a fixation that propelled this book.

Once I had the X-rays of my teeth I became curious. I reached out, paying fees to get copies of medical records, cold-calling doctors and offices, and filling in confusing and inaccessible forms. The University of Alberta told me that my psychological service history was contained in the archives, located on a pallet, and they physically retrieved, scanned, and e-mailed them to me. At the Grey Nuns Community Hospital, I paid thirty dollars to get the X-rays and CT scans of my lungs on CD and then bought a fifty-dollar disk drive to load them onto. Alberta Health Services charges twenty-five dollars for every twenty pages of material that is printed for you but doesn't have any way of telling you how much material there is, where to get it, or how long it might take.

I don't know if you know what it is like to live inside a body that continually tries to erase itself and to have a mind that you are not always privy to. I didn't find who I was in psych notes or release forms, but I did get to see what the system thought of me. In the medical industrial model there is a dehumanization that is so deeply embedded in disability that I could only fully grasp it through art.

I started writing this book in 2020, and it will be 2024 by the time it is in the world. By its release, I will have spent thousands of dollars on copays and even more in lost hours of pain and fatigue. The documents I'm working through cannot capture how much of my life has sprouted from the grief and joy of being disabled, nor how many more pages I could have spent trying to tell the whole story of disability, as complex as it is.

Some days, I don't know who I am without my labels: queer, disabled, woman, minority, marginalized, etc. But I exist. I am happy. I survive.

Part 1: disorder

(n.)

disability (n.)
1570s, want of power, strength, or ability from dis- + ability

disorder (n.)
(medical) an illness that causes a part of the body to stop functioning correctly

disease (n.)
a disorder of structure or function in a human, animal, or plant

i'll meet you there

tell me where it all goes down and I'll meet you there, I'll start the fight, at the intersections of inflamed aortas, and we'll offer a sacrifice, like the children offer teddy bears and flowers, at the place where even the doctor who outlived the last six doctors I had before him gave up

and when the teens give up it's a tragedy, and how can so many things be tragedies in one body when none of them kill you outright

no one wants to read a story if it has no ending

and if you'd told me to let go of my right hand, I would rather have become a headline, but I've had twenty-one months to think now and I've changed my mind

I'm willing to seal the deal or make a pact or swear an oath or see the neurologist and rheumatologist and the X-ray tech again, draw the blood two days in a row to get all ten vials, get call after call from three different doctors all telling me that it could be worse

and I know that too, I know that I am grateful for what this holy, this worship, this body still is, that it has a heart that beats even without all its platelets and red and white blood cells and insulin

but my multitudes are crying, quietly in a windowsill and loud in the shower when I cannot comb my hair and am left to cut out all the matted bits

and I still want this body, every second of it, even when I can't sign for the cheques they send me every time I talk about it

and I think it's funny that some people think heaven is just escaping from this body instead of fighting the world to teach yourself

how to love it.

an expectable or approved mental disorder

A mental disorder is ▓▓▓▓▓▓▓▓▓▓▓▓▓▓▓ significant
disturbance in an individual ▓▓▓▓▓▓▓▓▓▓▓▓ or
▓▓▓▓▓▓ that reflects a dysfunction in ▓▓▓▓▓▓▓▓▓▓▓
▓▓▓▓▓▓▓▓▓ underlying mental functioning. Mental
disorders are ▓▓▓▓▓▓▓▓▓▓▓▓▓▓▓▓▓ disability ▓
▓▓▓▓▓▓▓▓▓▓▓▓▓▓▓▓ A ▓▓▓
culturally approved response to a ▓▓▓▓ stressor ▓▓▓ such as ▓
death ▓▓▓▓▓ is not a mental disorder. Socially deviant behaviour
▓▓▓▓▓▓▓▓▓▓▓▓▓▓▓▓▓▓
▓▓▓▓▓▓▓▓▓▓▓▓▓ are not mental disorders ▓▓▓
▓▓▓▓▓▓▓▓▓▓▓▓▓▓▓▓▓▓
▓▓▓▓▓ A mental disorder is a ▓▓▓▓▓▓
▓▓▓▓▓▓▓▓▓▓▓▓▓▓▓▓▓▓
regulation, or ▓▓▓▓▓▓ a dysfunction in ▓▓▓▓▓▓
▓▓▓▓▓▓ processes ▓▓▓▓▓▓▓▓
Mental disorders are ▓▓▓▓▓▓▓▓▓▓▓ distress ▓
▓▓▓▓ in ▓▓▓▓▓▓▓▓▓ important activities. An
expectable or ▓▓▓▓ approved ▓▓▓▓
▓▓▓▓▓▓▓▓▓▓ mental disorder. ▓▓
deviant ▓▓▓▓▓▓▓▓▓▓▓▓▓ conflicts
▓▓ are ▓▓▓▓▓▓▓▓▓▓▓▓ not
▓▓▓▓▓▓▓▓▓▓▓▓▓ a dysfunction ▓▓
▓▓▓▓ as described
above. A mental disorder is ▓▓▓▓▓▓▓▓ clinically
▓▓▓▓▓▓▓▓ an individual's ▓▓▓▓▓▓
▓▓▓▓▓▓ dysfunction ▓▓▓▓▓
▓▓▓▓▓▓▓▓▓▓▓▓▓▓▓▓▓▓
▓ usually associated with ▓▓▓▓▓
▓▓▓▓▓▓▓▓▓▓▓▓▓▓▓▓▓▓
▓▓▓▓▓▓ a common stressor ▓▓▓▓▓
▓ loved one ▓ s ▓▓▓
▓▓▓▓▓▓▓▓▓▓▓▓▓▓▓▓▓▓
▓▓▓▓▓▓ are not mental disorders ▓▓▓
▓▓▓▓▓▓▓▓▓▓▓▓▓▓▓▓▓▓

or behaviour that reflects a dysfunction

Mental disorders
are usually

expectable

portrait of the artist as societal expectations of a GOOD DAY

DAYS Lost
On how many DAYS in the last month did your symptoms cause you to miss school or work or leave you unable to do your normal daily activities?

2–3

DAYS Unproductive
On how many DAYS in the last month did you feel so impaired by your symptoms that even though you went to school or work, your productivity was reduced?

5–6

I could probably
be GOOD
 if I had an extra
[84–108 days]
 a year to do it.

but ~~I'm sorry~~
~~*it's not my fault*~~
I am not a GOOD DAY
I am not even GOOD

Generalized Anxiety Disorder 300.02 (F41.1)

are you happy?

    why?
    (short answer, please)

    why not?
    (bonus question)

re: what do emotions do for you?

What do emotions do for you? What does *E•MO•TION* (third studio album by Canadian singer and songwriter Carly Rae Jepsen) do for you? What does a *natural instinctive state of mind* do for you? What does (Destiny's Child's) "Emotion" do for you? (What does *destiny* do for you?) What does (@MariahCareyvEVO)'s "Emotions" do for you? *Emotions are biologically based psychological states.* Emotions have *no scientific consensus* on a definition. How do you define emotion? How do you define the worst parts of yourself?

How do you define the day you found the letter, a prelude to a cold body, from someone who was supposed to love you, saying goodbye? How do you write that same letter, fifteen years later, saying goodbye?

What do letters do for you?

What do suicide notes do for you?

Is it a suicide note if it starts with "Dear Reader" and ends with one of *The 9 Best Emotional TV Shows Guaranteed to Make You Cry*? Does ET get to go home because they want to, or because they simply don't fit in anymore, and their mother told them this would happen if they went outside or played too long, and maybe coming home to your mother is a way of showing emotion too. What do mothers do for you? Write it down now. Write a book. Call it *E•MO•TIONs* (after Carly Ray Jepsen). It'll sell a million copies and buy you nothing but silence at Christmas dinner.

have you been googling?

☰ Portrait of the Artist

Article

From Wikipedia, the free encyclopedia

From a body masquerading as the future

> For other uses, see *beautiful* (disambiguation).
> Not to be confused with *a life not worth living*.

in a lab, a scientist created a paint so black that seeing it defied any
known understanding of darkness. Virginia Woolf, confined to her
bed by no observable Newtonian epiphany, reached across a continent
of language and time to tell me that this darkness has a name (Nisha,
meaning "night" in Sanskrit, *nisha*), that it looks like me and doesn't,
that it's inside and outside all the time, that it does not need to be still or
contained across the operas of silence. we are our own centre of gravity,
and the world around us is falling in too, caving to make us pebbles
of burning gas, heated cores of the anxiety that pulls me to the centre of
this bed for so many days that even the sun starts to run circles around
me

Further Excuses
- *we did everything we could (and charged you for it)*
- *insurance won't cover it*
- *the wait-list is eighteen months, but it takes only ten for approval of
  your own medical assistance in dying (Canada)*

I'm a good one, because I won't complain about the nine appointments
I have this month, and I'll fit into the hospital robes like da Vinci fit
his, I'll drink enough water for the blood tests and the ultrasounds, I
won't complain about the soreness inside of my uterus, or the press of
the probes that tell me my wrists are fluid free, I won't cry, I won't cry, I
won't cry, I'll take off my aging engagement ring for the X-rays, and I will
lie so still and pray that the next MRI (see: *magnetic resonance imaging*)
will be worth it

they tell me that the line between crying wolf and self-help is thin, and
most of us are on the side with the blue pens and not the red, most of
us are on the side of falling water, the printer's requisition ink, the gas
stations and the parking tickets and the vomit on an empty stomach

they told me the CBT+ was worth it, the talk therapy was worth it,
staying quiet and arriving on time was worth it every time

even though I waited a year for the system to consider me worth it,
having two bad days would expel me from my own treatment, and
getting better on a doctor's day shift is only the mercy the government will
pay for

it gets so quiet sometimes. it gets so quiet that I think the
pharmacist who gives me emergency salbutamol but only thirty days of
lorazepam (see: *benzos are bad controlled substances*) thinks there is a
good and a bad way to die

they tell me "wait until you bleed through your mouth and help will
come"
they tell me that if I bleed through the prescription pad or the ovarian
cysts or the Ozempic overdose it is working

they tell me that the way my heart tightens without any sign of plaque or thrombosis is okay, that crying in the T&T is okay, that crying at the Shoppers (see: *medical price-fixing*) is okay, as if the loved ones who care enough to text aren't being pinned to boards like butterflies too, as if the spectacle of my illness is power, like the flourishing kingdom of my bed is power, like the grief of staying "home" when no one wants you to leave it is power, and like saving yourself is

this article is a stub. this article is not an ending. this article is a wish. this this this article is

cognitive behavioural therapy: session 6

She became quite emotional. What does emotion do for her? We can't help but wonder, as doctors with her best interests in mind. She shared a painful experience in front of strangers she dislikes. She dislikes us. We can tell, as doctors. She is a painful experience too, a body peeled out of a myelin sheath like a summer corn husk. A fist of sheaths, holding her up by her legs, or her spine, or somewhere bodies go when they are made to bare themselves to other suicidal girls in group therapy. Her strings are showing. The man from session 1 does not come back, and we wonder, as doctors, what his problem is, if the room was too small, not enough things to throw or throats to break, the smell of corn syrup running down bare legs too much. We are pleased to see her open up, from uvula to phalanges, from husk to seed. We are pleased, as doctors, to split her open with a scalpel made of psychiatric mind games and reinforced steel. We are pleased. She has nowhere to go but to participate more in the group.

Date: March 4, 2013

UNIVERSITY | MENTAL
WELLNESS | HEALTH
SERVICES | CENTRE

Client's name: ████████

Session number: 1

Client stated that she finds it very difficult to feel happy ████████████ ████████████████████

Date: March 20, 2013

UNIVERSITY | MENTAL
WELLNESS | HEALTH
SERVICES | CENTRE

Client's name: ███████

Session number: 2

Client did not appear to have any ideas ███████████████
██████

Date: April 3, 2013

UNIVERSITY | MENTAL
WELLNESS | HEALTH
SERVICES | CENTRE

Client's name: ████████

Session number: 3

Client was 15 minutes late for session.

Client stated her desire to keep ███████████████████████ developing depression.

Date: April 18, 2013

UNIVERSITY | MENTAL
WELLNESS | HEALTH
SERVICES | CENTRE

Client's name: ██████████

Session number: 4

Client stated that she has found herself ████████████

████████████████ helpless in her emotions and described a
panic attack she had ██████████████████████████

████████ when describing ██████████████ her life.

Date: Aug 8, 2013

UNIVERSITY | MENTAL
WELLNESS | HEALTH
SERVICES | CENTRE

Client's name: ███████

Session number: 7

Client stated that she has had rapid mood swings ████████████
Client is quite concerned.

Therapist reassured client that she would be ████████████
████████████

████████ referred to a psychiatrist.

Date: August 8, 2013

UNIVERSITY | MENTAL
WELLNESS | HEALTH
SERVICES | CENTRE

Referral to Psychiatric Services

Client's Name: ~~NISHA PATEL~~

Client stated that she experiences regular and intense changes in mood client describes client notes client considers client consultanted client is on the wait-list client strongly feels she needs to be assessed and on medication client experiences intense suicidal ideation client stated that there is little that holds her back client states client will

INBOX *This is a*

☐ mhcentre   INBOX Appointment Reminder - This is a fri
☐ mhcentre   INBOX Appointment Reminder - This is a fri
☐ mhcentre   INBOX Appointment Reminder - This is a fri
☐ mhcentre   INBOX Appointment Reminder - This is a fri
☐ mhcentre   INBOX Appointment Reminder - This is a fri
☐ mhcentre   INBOX Appointment Reminder - This is a fri
☐ mhcentre   INBOX Appointment Reminder - This is a fri
☐ mhcentre   INBOX Appointment Reminder - This is a fri
☐ mhcentre   INBOX Appointment Reminder - This is a fri
☐ mhcentre   INBOX Appointment Reminder - This is a fri
☐ mhcentre   INBOX Appointment Reminder - This is a fri
☐ mhcentre   INBOX Appointment Reminder - This is a fri
☐ mhcentre   INBOX Appointment Reminder - This is a fri
☐ mhcentre   INBOX Appointment Reminder - This is a fri
☐ mhcentre   INBOX Appointment Reminder - This is a fri
☐ mhcentre   INBOX Appointment Reminder - This is a fri
☐ mhcentre   INBOX Appointment Reminder - This is a fri
☐ mhcentre   INBOX Appointment Reminder - This is a fri
☐ mhcentre   INBOX Appointment Reminder - This is a fri
☐ mhcentre   INBOX Appointment Reminder - This is a fri
☐ mhcentre   INBOX Appointment Reminder - This is a fri
☐ mhcentre   INBOX Appointment Reminder - This is a fri
☐ mhcentre   INBOX Appointment Reminder - This is a fri
☐ mhcentre   INBOX Appointment Reminder - This is a fri
☐ mhcentre   INBOX Appointment Reminder - This is a fri
☐ mhcentre   INBOX Appointment Reminder - This is a fri
☐ mhcentre   INBOX Appointment Reminder - This is a fri
☐ mhcentre   INBOX Appointment Reminder - This is a fri
☐ mhcentre   INBOX Appointment Reminder - This is a fri
☐ mhcentre   INBOX Appointment Reminder - This is a fri

Pleasant Event List
(Emotion Regulation Handout 16)

1. Working on my car
2. Planning a career
3. Getting out of (paying down) debt
4. Collecting things (baseball cards, coins, stamps, rocks, shells, etc.)
5. Going on vacation
6. Thinking how it will be when I finish school
7. Recycling old items
8. Going on a date
9. Relaxing
10. Going to or watching a movie
11. Jogging, walking
12. Thinking, "I have done a full day's work" ✕
13. Listening to music
14. Thinking about past parties
15. Buying household gadgets
16. Lying in the sun
17. Planning a career change
18. Laughing
19. Thinking about past trips
20. Listening to other people
21. Reading magazines or newspapers
22. Engaging in hobbies (stamp collecting, model building, etc.)
23. Spending an evening with good friends
24. Planning a day's activities
25. Meeting new people
26. Remembering beautiful scenery
27. Saving money ✕
28. Going home from work
29. Eating
30. Practicing karate, judo, yoga
31. Thinking about retirement
32. Repairing things around the house
33. Working on machinery (cars, boats, etc.)
34. Remembering the words and deeds of loving people
35. Wearing shocking clothes
36. Having quiet evenings
37. Taking care of my plants
38. Buying, selling stock
39. Going swimming
40. Having quiet evenings
41. Taking care of my plants
42. Buying, selling stock
43. Doodling
44. Exercising
45. Collecting old things
46. Going to a party
47. Thinking about buying things

12.

the first time I said it out loud, I had to stifle the movement of my gut as it tried to exit my throat. the words were a captive made free, bruised and battered, after a long isolation. they were famished words, lean and thin and barely there. but they still spoke when I called their names. still echoed in the silence that longed to be filled with my own sobs.

I have done a full day's work.

if I put it in quotation marks you'll know that I said it.

"I have done a full day's work."

is it true?

48. Playing golf
49. Playing soccer
50. Flying kites
51. Having discussions with friends
52. Having family get-togethers
53. Riding a bike or motorbike
54. Running track
55. Going camping
56. Singing around the house
57. Arranging flowers
58. Practising religion (church, praying, etc.)
59. Organizing tools
60. Going to the beach
61. Thinking, "I'm an okay person"   X
62. Having a day with nothing to do   X
63. Going to class reunions
64. Going skating, skateboarding, rollerblading
65. Going sailing or motorboating
66. Travelling or going on vacations
67. Painting
68. Doing something spontaneously
69. Doing needlepoint, crewel, etc.
70. Sleeping
71. Driving
72. Entertaining, giving parties
73. Going to clubs (garden clubs, Parents Without Partners, etc.)
74. Thinking about getting married
75. Going hunting
76. Singing with groups
77. Flirting
78. Playing musical instruments
79. Doing arts and crafts
80. Making a gift for someone X
81. Buying/downloading music
82. Watching boxing, wrestling
83. Planning parties
84. Cooking
85. Going hiking
86. Writing (books, poems, articles)
87. Sewing
88. Buying clothes
89. Going out to dinner
90. Working
91. Discussing books; going to a book club
92. Sightseeing
93. Getting a manicure/pedicure or facial
94. Going to the beauty parlour

83.

in high school, I was voted Most Likely to Defeat Bowser. in high school, I was voted Students' Union president. I was a Seminar on the United Nations and International Affairs scholarship recipient. I had ten different nail polishes from Sephora. I was a future lawyer, or politician, or anything but a prelude to a love letter to the dead. I was not dead, or dying, or dying to meet my future. I was a list of 228 pleasant events. I was a list of reasons why the doctors admitted me to the psych ward. I was a day with no triggers but parking my car. I was a party full of flirting and arts and crafts and hiking. I was a beauty parlour on Sunday. an early morning coffee, before riding a motorbike to a painting of a kite on the beach. I was an arrangement of flowers, none of them white. none of them for sympathy.

95. Early morning coffee and newspaper
96. Playing tennis
97. Kissing
98. Watching my children (play)
99. Thinking, "I have a lot more going for me than most people"
100. Going to plays and concerts
101. Daydreaming
102. Planning to go (back) to school
103. Thinking about sex
104. Going for a drive
105. Refinishing furniture
106. Watching TV
107. Making lists of tasks
108. Walking in the woods (or at the waterfront)
109. Buying gifts
110. Completing a task
111. Going to a spectator sport (auto racing, horse racing)
112. Teaching
113. Photography
114. Going fishing
115. Thinking about pleasant events
116. Staying on a diet
117. Playing with animals
118. Flying a plane
119. Reading fiction
120. Acting
121. Being alone
122. Writing diary entries or letters
123. Cleaning
124. Reading non-fiction
125. Taking children places
126. Dancing
127. Weightlifting
128. Going on a picnic
129. Thinking, "I did that pretty well," after doing something
130. Meditating, yoga
131. Having lunch with a friend
132. Going to the mountains
130. Playing hockey
133. Working with clay or pottery
134. Glass-blowing
135. Going skiing
136. Dressing up
137. Reflecting on how I've improved
138. Buying small things for myself (perfume, golf balls, etc.)
139. Talking on the phone
140. Going to museums
141. Thinking religious thoughts

141.

thinking *I am God* is not the same as believing in one; my gods moved
and held mountains
born of prison and kingdom unreachable

who am I to think I am reborn of blue flesh or elephant trunk?

but I feel for those who have never once thought themselves invincible
never walked without shoes down a sidewalk hoping to take a running
start at flight
never lived with a mind full of possibilities for naming stars
words like *episode* and *disorder* mean nothing
as you are freed from all limitations of human body
and become one with the clouds, or the sun, or yourself.

I believe in nothing, not even my blood, to save me.

142. Lighting candles
143. Whitewater canoeing/rafting
144. Going bowling
145. Doing woodworking
146. Fantasizing about the future
147. Taking ballet/tap dancing classes
148. Debating
149. Sitting in a sidewalk café
150. Having an aquarium
151. Participating in "living history" events
152. Knitting
153. Doing crossword puzzles
154. Shooting pool
155. Getting a massage

156. Saying, "I love you" ✕
157. Playing catch, taking batting practice
158. Shooting baskets
159. Seeing and/or showing photos
160. Thinking about my good qualities
161. Solving riddles mentally
162. Having a political discussion
163. Buying books
164. Taking a sauna or a steam bath
165. Checking out garage sales
166. Thinking about having a family
167. Thinking about happy moments in my childhood
168. Splurging
169. Going horseback riding
170. Doing something new
171. Working on jigsaw puzzles
172. Playing cards
173. Thinking, "I'm a person who can cope"
174. Taking a nap
175. Figuring out my favourite scent
176. Making a card and giving it to someone I care about
177. Instant messaging/texting someone
178. Playing a board game (e.g., Monopoly, Life, Clue, Sorry!)
179. Putting on my favourite piece of clothing
180. Making a smoothie and drinking it slowly
181. Putting on makeup
182. Thinking about a friend's good qualities
183. Completing something I feel great about
184. Surprising someone with a favour
185. Surfing the Internet
186. Playing video games
187. E-mailing friends
188. Going walking or sledding in a snowfall
189. Getting a haircut

156.

Katherine caught me off guard once.

"do you love your mother?"

190. Installing new software
191. Buying a CD or music on iTunes
192. Watching sports on TV
193. Taking care of my pets
194. Doing volunteer service
195. Watching stand-up comedy on YouTube
196. Working in my garden
197. Participating in a public performance (e.g., a flash mob)
198. Blogging
199. Fighting for a cause
200. Conducting experiments
201. Expressing my love to someone
202. Going on field trips, exploring (hiking away from known routes)
203. Going downtown or to a shopping mall
204. Going to a fair, carnival, circus, zoo, or amusement park
205. Going to the library
206. Joining or forming a band
207. Learning to do something new
208. Listening to the sounds of nature
209. Looking at the moon or stars
210. Outdoor work (cutting or chopping wood, farmwork)
211. Playing organized sports (baseball, football, Frisbee, soccer, tennis)
212. Playing in the sand, a stream, the grass; kicking leaves, pebbles, etc.
213. Protesting social, political, or environmental conditions
214. Reading cartoons or comics
215. Reading sacred works
216. Rearranging or redecorating my room or the house
217. Selling or trading something
218. Snowmobiling or riding a dune buggy / ATV
219. Social networking
220. Soaking in the bathtub
221. Learning or speaking a foreign language
222. Talking on the phone
223. Composing or arranging songs or music
224. Thrift store shopping
225. Using computers
226. Visiting people who are sick, shut in, or in trouble
227. Other:
228. Other:

Session 6

CBT+ Notes - Session 6

She became quite emotional during homework review, as she shared a painful experience. We are pleased to see her open up and participate more in the group.

Distress Tolerance Worksheet 9 - Radical Acceptance

WHAT I NEED TO ACCEPT
(Acceptance, 0–5)

_____

_____

_____

_____

_____

_____

Sometimes people who leave don't want to come back. (2)

_____

_____

_____

_____

_____

_____

_____

_____

portrait of the artist as an episode of the
TV series House

it's not lupus   it's not the head trauma   it's manic-depression
it's not lupus   it's not the head trauma   it's manic-depression
it's not lupus   it's not the head trauma   it's manic-depression
it's not lupus   it's not t**DATE 15 - Oct 2015** it's manic-depression
it's not lupus   it's not the head trauma   it's manic-depression
it's not lupus   it's not the head trauma   it's manic-depression
it's not lupus   it's not the head trauma   it's manic-depression
it's not lupus   it's not the head trauma   it's manic-depression
it's not lupus   it's not the head trauma   it's manic-depression
it's not lupus   it's not the head trauma   it's manic-depression
it's not lupus   it's not the head trauma   it's manic-depression
it's not lupus   it's not the head trauma   it's manic-depression
it's not lupus   it's not the head trauma *patient actually suspected that she had bipolar*
it's not lupus   it's not the head trauma   it's manic-depression
it's not lupus   it's not the head trauma   it's manic-depression
it's not lupus   it's not the head trauma   it's manic-depression
it's not lupus   it's not the head trauma   it's manic-depression
it's not lupus   it's not the head trauma   it's manic-depression
it's not lupus   it's not the head trauma   it's manic-depression
it's not lupus   it's not the head trauma   it's manic-depression
it's not lupus   it's not the head trauma   it's manic-depression
it's not lupus   it's not the head trauma   it's manic-depression
it's not lupus   it's not the head trauma   it's manic-depression
it's not lupus   it's not the head trauma   it's manic-depression
it's not lupus   it's not the head trauma   it's manic-depression
it's not lupus   it's not the head trauma   it's manic-depression

Encounter Date: 07/02/2017

Client is still finding it difficult to concentrate and states even working for two hours is "draining"

draining

I grew up when *Twilight* hit the box office. Some call it a phenomenon, but what is a monster if not just desire made flesh?

Of three things, I am certain.

First, I remember what it is like to have looked forward to my body.

Second, there is some part of me—and I don't know how potent that part might be—that wants to be free of my body.

And third, I unconditionally and irrevocably want to stay in this body. I want to love this body. I want to love you, in this body, forever.

Encounter Date: 07/02/2017:
client is prone to nightmares

without fail, seven days a week, the dosette goes round and round, the sevenths spilling into more sevenths until they form a spiral staircase into the base of my skull, except this time the steps are made of chalky pink. my feet slip on the penultimate step and I fall into a pit of purple and blue, the colours of my blood before I've breathed life into it, and in the bottom of my body I am one thing in a large room of nothing, I have no grounding and I am surrounded by sounds, this one of myself crying in my preteen house, the other, my mother crying where she thinks no one can hear, until the sounds split into sevenths. I'm swallowing people, all seven I used to live with, all disappointed, and the ground beneath me is smoke, the stars above me are my own pupils, and climbing into my brain are the doctors who think I am too heavy, and maybe I am. because now I'm falling down my throat, the walls are stuck with Ativan, and I dig my nails into my wet esophagus. I climb my way out of my own body, and all that happens next is a dream in seven parts, one for each day of the week, to convince myself I am still alive.

Encounter Date: 07/02/2017

States she feels guilty "over everything" and has difficulty turning off her racing thoughts.

drowning

Team building, but make it physical. Make it orange and blue, like the Oilers, make it *Survivor* or *Fear Factor*, me and the elements. We're indoors at a gymnastics arena and I'm overweight in a group of tennis players and golfers who like their whisky on the rocks. I enter the foam pit and attempt to cross like a water strider, all legs, and man, my ex always said I had killer thighs. Except this time I sink and I have no idea how time stops and goes on for too long at the same time, because one second I am doing fine, I am breathing, and the next I'm in a fucking foam pit without oxygen and I am screaming for help. I am drowning like I once saw my brother drown next to me at eight, and that time I didn't do a thing. And I forgive them, my new colleagues who have never seen a panic attack before, because neither have I. My brother made it out without me. I cry and an eighteen-year-old gymnast pulls me out. My first time panicking, and it lingers. My new skin itches.

Part 2: disease

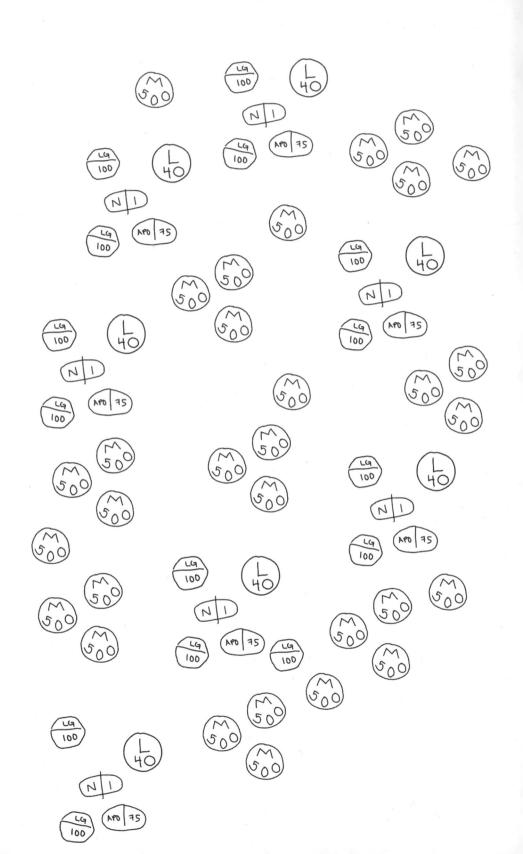

the curse of the Kohinoor

the curse of the Kohinoor diamond tells us
that all empires who covet it will fall

but when the British East India Company forces
all 105 carats of it into the centre of the coronation crown
Queen Elizabeth calls it merely *heavy*

the way the intergenerational epigenetics of colonial famine are *heavy*

the way the shortened lifespans of my grandfather
       and grandmother
       and grandmother
       and mother-in-law
       and father-in-law
       and father
       and aunt
       and aunt
       and uncle
       and uncle

are *heavy.*

the Kohinoor is considered so valuable
that it cannot be assessed

but I know
       it weighs one-fourth of my pancreas,
       six days of insulin,
       and one-fifteenth of my grandfather's seizing heart

it is worth less than
        AstraZeneca
        than Eli Lilly
        than Sanofi
        and Sanofi-Aventis
so if you give me a choice between being cursed by the Kohinoor
and a cure for diabetes

        we will have different definitions of what is priceless.

my father's daughter

pen in hand, my thighs a new canvas
      pointillism

I've never been precise about anything
the needle is quiet
my body is not

the pharmacy gives free sharps boxes if you ask nicely

(I am the hazard in the room)

some days I wish I'd said no
told the doctors that my pancreas was lying, playing dead
run the tests again
my body just needed a break

wish I'd told him there are worse things than death
like a body that works the way it's supposed to turning into
a body that does not

I didn't ask for this
illness makes me a tourist somewhere I called home

I feel like I'm always leaving my body
when the needle enters
      goodbye, and hello to the next twenty-four hours

tomorrow night, before bed
I will write on the oldest canvas of all:
      the skin of a beast tied together around a spine I can't feel
      without puncture

how to spend $13.25/day

by wanting to wake, again.

refills

I think the pharmacist pities me when I cry at the till. I'm sorry, I want to say, but instead all that comes out is *I'll just take thirty days.*

inject/protect/take/do not break/do not consume/ do not stop/avoid/keep

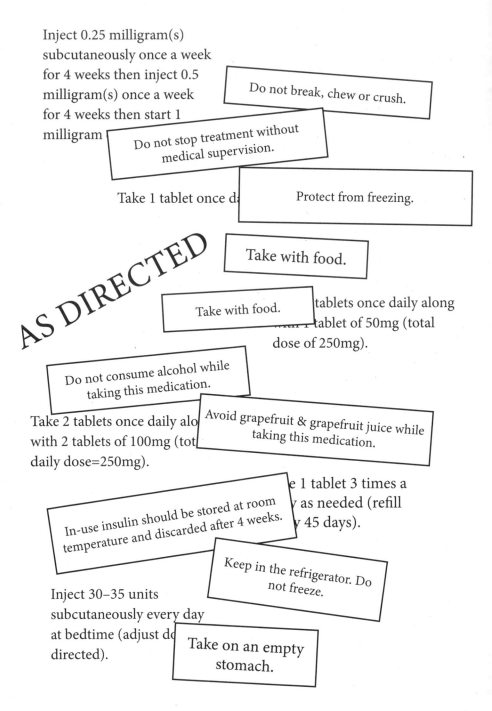

Inject 0.25 milligram(s) subcutaneously once a week for 4 weeks then inject 0.5 milligram(s) once a week for 4 weeks then start 1 milligram

Do not break, chew or crush.

Do not stop treatment without medical supervision.

Take 1 tablet once da

Protect from freezing.

Take with food.

AS DIRECTED

Take with food.

tablets once daily along
tablet of 50mg (total dose of 250mg).

Do not consume alcohol while taking this medication.

Take 2 tablets once daily alo
with 2 tablets of 100mg (tot
daily dose=250mg).

Avoid grapefruit & grapefruit juice while taking this medication.

e 1 tablet 3 times a
as needed (refill
45 days).

In-use insulin should be stored at room temperature and discarded after 4 weeks.

Keep in the refrigerator. Do not freeze.

Inject 30–35 units subcutaneously every day at bedtime (adjust d directed).

Take on an empty stomach.

Verification of Disability

To Whom it May Concern:

Accessibility Resources (AR) provides individualized services to students with disabilities to support them in successfully meeting their educational goals. Students accessing services through AR are required to provide documentation of a permanent health condition or long-term disability.

1. Nature of the Disability
Provide the specific diagnosis(es) and describe the nature of the disability(ies). In the case of mental health diagnoses, please include reference to the DSM-5 criteria.

      Bipolar disorder, type II

2. Verification of Disability
Is the diagnosis(es):

          Temporary? (Please indicate approximate time to return to full function)

     X   Permanent? (i.e., not likely to fully resolve within the individual's life time)

questions for Google at 4 a.m.

Q   are there any disabled superheroes?   X

Google Search   I'm Feeling Lucky

If The Incredible Hulk was Disabled

he would have to fit on the leather couch
as the doctor read out
312.34 (F63.81): Intermittent Explosive Disorder
and he would refuse to accept it, neither
the rapid onset with no prodromal period
nor the observation that his behaviour violated societal norms

he would certainly need more therapy
perhaps group, like I did for ten weeks
seated next to the girl who wanted to walk into traffic
I've seen The Hulk walk into traffic
without getting in trouble for it
and no one asks him if he's having a bad day
no one asks him if he's on his period when he looks a little green
or stressed out, or angry
no one sends him to the psych ward against his will
or straps him to a gurney without shoes like the rest of us
because men are allowed to be angry all the time
beastly men, men of width and precarity

> I was an episode of my father's anger
> I was a flicker in the memories of my mother's wars

and when I was a girl, I was angry all the time
bitten tongues bleeding fury into the energy of the universe
the summation of my limbs an elongated rage

until I grew into a woman who could be called *high functioning*
could surpass my potential, dazzle the others, feign normality

which is to say that if I met The Hulk now I would whisper

> Incredible, huh? *that's what they call me*

on the night Gwen Stacy dies

on the night Gwen Stacy dies Peter Parker comes home without a single drop of blood on his hands, which is why he doesn't sleep, or bathe, or eat for days, because surviving long enough to see everyone you love leave does that to a person

and there's nothing amazing about it, no one sends postcards to New York, and maybe Peter Parker stays in bed too long, lets time dampen the pits of his spandex, and if he takes it off he isn't at fault, so he keeps it on, and he doesn't cry

until the teenage girls in the psych wards remind him through their bars that there are still more Gwens worth saving, and Peter Parker knows this but still wishes his heart wasn't as delicate as a spider's web

wishes it didn't catch the worst of his love and the best of his failure in one moment, when a woman who was once a girl stilled in his arms and he had to pretend he was someone they didn't call a hero

even the hero looks like a villain when dead girls fall from the sky

and maybe villains get a bad rap after all, because who hasn't felt an anger so deep it threatens both the rats in the sewers as well as the lilacs and the pansies

if roses were all thorn Peter Parker would buy them every day

he'd trim their leaves and leave their stems to hold up tiny heads of buds that would never bloom, like the girl now a ghost, like the boy now a man, snap their necks like his folly snapped hers, and this time he'd bead a single drop of blood

and it would fall to the pavement without a sound and release him from his guilt, again.

Significant Investigations

Alberta Health Services
Covenant Health

Uncomplicated Short Stay Discharge Summary or Physician Information Sheet

Admission Date   Feb 2/17

Most Responsible Diagnosis

                        1. Bipolar ii depressed episode

Significant Investigations / Relevant diagnostic results / Course in hospital:

                        1. follow-up @ crisis team

Discharge Date   Feb 2/17

Disposition: X Home   Against Advice   Deceased

@ *crisis team follow-up*

GNCH MENTAL HEALTH
Addiction and Mental Health
Grey Nuns Psychiatric Stabilization Team
Progress Notes

28/3/2017

Client seen for follow-up.

Has an appointment with Dr. ██████████ in early June.

June 2017

"I think you just have poor self-control"

already attempted unsuccessfully

INBOX Aug 19, 2014, 9:27 a.m.

Hello ███

███
█████████████████████████████████████ you already
attempted this course twice
unsuccessfully.

███████████████████████████████████ if you want to
attempt this course for a third time you will need permission ████████
███
███
████████
███
█████████████████████████ ensure that you will be successful in
this attempt.
███
██████████████████████████ ███████████████████████
████ failure ███████████████████████████████████
████████ will result in your discontinuation ████████████████

███
███████████████████████████████████

████████

your sincere dedication

INBOX May 25, 2015, 4:15 p.m.

██

███

███

███

Unfortunately, you did not achieve this GPA in your final year of studies and were deemed ineligible for this competition.

███

████████████████████████ we wish you the best ████████████████

████████████

MAID *in heaven*

The law no longer requires that a person's death be reasonably foreseeable
to be eligible for medical assistance in dying. Which means, of course,
that the want of death is not an anomaly anymore, but a legally
sanctioned whim. Which means, of course, that we will stop calling
suicide a tragedy. Which means, of course, that we will understand that
killing yourself and letting the state kill you are discernibly different.
Which means, of course, of course, that no disabled person will ever be so
starved of the means of living that they choose medically assisted death
over their fulfilling and state-sanctioned lives. The teens are rewriting
their Tumblr posts. The teens are playing Nirvana on repeat. The teens are
making infographics. The state posts on Twitter that mental illness cannot
be the sole reason for wanting to die, that there are safeguards, like school
counsellors and university professors, in place, but the teens laugh until
they cry when they hear this. No lawmaker finds this legislation funny.
No lawmaker has ever heard the word *comorbidity*. No lawmaker has ever
stood barefoot on speckled tile and wondered whether swallowing the
Ambien or running was worth it. No lawmaker has ever sat at a dinner
table with six pills in hand and two needles ready to go and thought to
themselves, *It will only ever be a last resort to ask for medical assistance in
dying. I myself am fully capable of asking for medical assistance in dying.
I myself have everything I need. I myself want the option of but will never
have to choose medical assistance in dying. No one will ever coerce me.
The doctor will always listen. The psychiatrist is always available without
a wait-list. The car has an airbag and the bridges have nets and the trains
don't go fast enough. If I want my own death it is because I have everything
I need and am in need no more. This isn't about pain, we swear. This is a
perfect system in which my body, free of its own terminality, gives full and
informed consent.* We surveyed a thousand Canadians and most of them
are not even a memory now. Most of those who died in another type of
pain died the way they wanted to—without headlines, at their own hands
instead of the gun lobby's. Most of them chose freedom—true, God-
given freedom—to die and did not live in the province with the highest
rent in Canada. Doctors receive only a flat fee of $200 for performing the
procedure, and we all know that no doctor makes so little that this would

be an incentive. Please note that all terminal and non-terminal illnesses eventually end in death anyway, so no, we have no problem sleeping at night. Please note that missed appointments have a no-show fee of $50.

37%

37% of those with bipolar disorder have substance abuse disorders

according to the Government of Canada, the pharmaceutical sector made 27 billion dollars in 2017

you could have died

"you can buy anything you want"
"$15/tab is too much, you got ripped off"
"it's usually $60/gram"
"you can't get addicted to weed"
"I crushed it up and snorted it"
"when are you coming home"
"I went to bed at 6 a.m. and left at 7 a.m."
"when are you coming home"
"no one trips for eight hours"
"I wasn't feeling it so I took two more grams"
"when are you coming home"
"the tea will help"
"I quit cold and we had nothing in common anymore"
"I had to get out of there, I was wasting my life"
"I watched it ruin his life"
"what were you thinking"
"you could have died"
"I want you to come home"

r/bipolar

 You make a deal with the devil. You restart your life at the beginning of adulthood. Your bipolar, addictions, and other mental illnesses are gone. In exchange, your soul. Would you do it?

r/bipolar + Posted 1 year ago

26 comments

high risk

Suicide risk is high in bipolar II disorder.
Suicide risk is high in bipolar II disorder.
~~Suicide risk is high in bipolar II disorder.~~
Suicide risk is high in bipolar II disorder.
Suicide risk is high in bipolar II disorder.
~~Suicide risk is high in bipolar II disorder.~~
Suicide risk is high in bipolar II disorder.
Suicide risk is high in bipolar II disorder.
~~Suicide risk is high in bipolar II disorder.~~
Suicide risk is high in bipolar II disorder.
Suicide risk is high in bipolar II disorder.
~~Suicide risk is high in bipolar II disorder.~~
Suicide risk is high in bipolar II disorder.
Suicide risk is high in bipolar II disorder.
~~Suicide risk is high in bipolar II disorder.~~
Suicide risk is high in bipolar II disorder.
Suicide risk is high in bipolar II disorder.
~~Suicide risk is high in bipolar II disorder.~~
Suicide risk is high in bipolar II disorder.
Suicide risk is high in bipolar II disorder.
~~Suicide risk is high in bipolar II disorder.~~
Suicide risk is high in bipolar II disorder.
Suicide risk is high in bipolar II disorder.
~~Suicide risk is high in bipolar II disorder.~~

approximately one-third of individuals with bipolar II disorder report a lifetime history of a suicide attempt

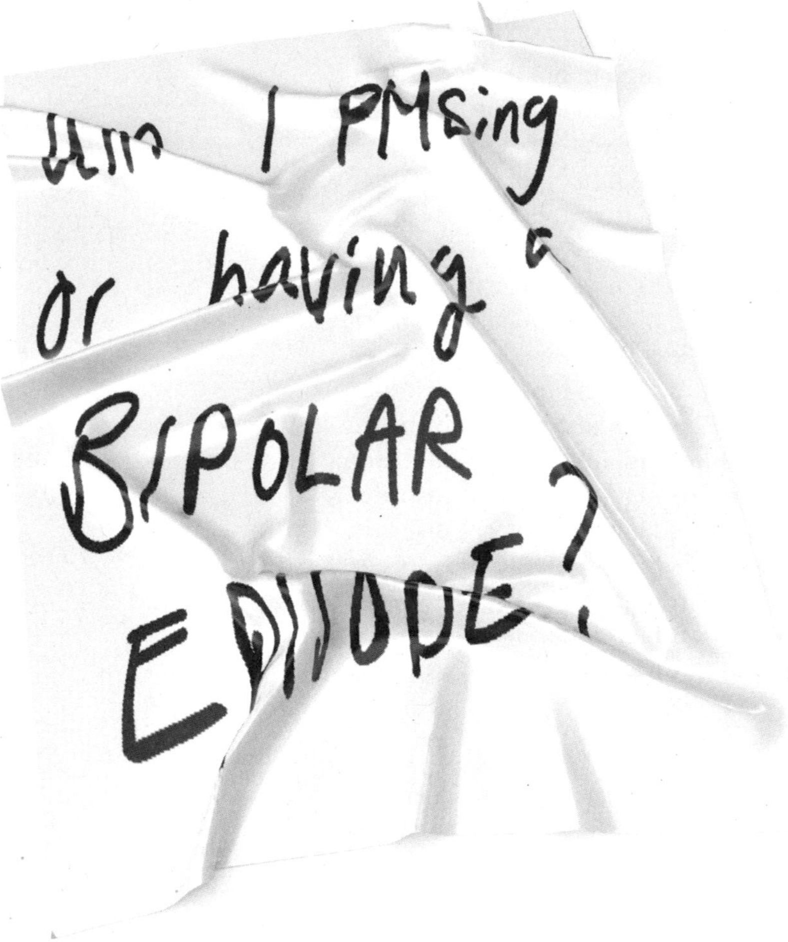
I PMSing
or having
BIPOLAR
EPISODE?

concussions are caused by a blow to the head

I don't look like an athlete or a dancer, although I used to be one. And I'm what my outpatient psychiatrist called high functioning. I'm very good at some things: public speaking, planning parties, writing poems. But I can't memorize performances, I can't get up too quickly, and I can't go on the Mindbender at West Edmonton Mall four times in a row anymore.

Here's what I know: brain injuries change people. Concussions, or mild traumatic brain injuries, are denoted by any force that shakes your brain up inside your skull. Think of your brain as a gumball. Each time you collide with a soccer ball or sidewalk, it's like you're biting down just a little—the shell of the gumball starts to crack. Sometimes, your brain heals quickly, in seven to ten days. But for some people, concussions are life altering, where a single blow changes your processing and behaviour—the gum is chewed up. For years, we thought concussions did not leave marks or evidence on MRIs and scans. I've heard that having three or more can lead to a serious condition called postconcussive syndrome. I've had eleven. My gumball is getting a little stringy.

And those are the ones I remember. My primary source material is polluted, tainted by imperfect memory. And although I tell myself that memory loss is common, I still feel the frustration—what hurts? Everything. How did it happen? I don't know. After my first concussion, I was happy to skip class. After my sixth, I lost consciousness. Then came the migraines. By my eleventh, I started losing language. Words and feelings aching together.

Concussions have affected the way I think, move, and sleep. And some of these changes don't go away in two weeks.

Concussion signs and symptoms may include:

Headache
Mental fogginess
Loss of consciousness
Amnesia
Confusion or difficulty concentrating
Personality changes
Sleep disturbances
Dizziness
Ringing in ears
Nausea and vomiting
Slurred speech
Fatigue
Sensitivity to light and noise

"How many concussions is too many?"

eleven

"Somehow the magic number for concussions became three, even though no one is sure how or why. The research doesn't back it up."

I've had ~~eleven~~.

13

Concussions feel like:

-a verbal blindfold
-gauze around the tongue
-aching
-seconds split into seconds and seconds and seconds
-faltering
-viscous spinal fluid
-the need for more time to do less

portrait of the artist as a series of cumulative blows to the head (3-D)

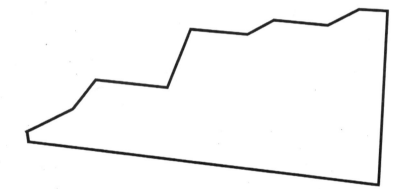

Brain tissue taken from dead vets and footballers shows scarring from concussions, resulting in tighter folds. More protein. Tighter squiggles.

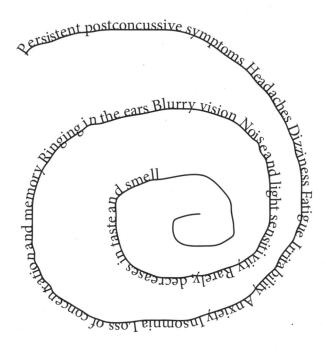

I remember the sound and the smell and the sight—green artificial turf. Blue Adidas. The musk of sweaty knee socks. The sports concussions were the most acceptable. And the lights, whiter than I'd ever seen them, white as the tunnel's end, suddenly whiting out everything else around me. The lights are the most familiar—they have revisited me every injury since. Some days, if I move too quickly from the desk or the car, I get flashes that they're still haunting my body, that I am their chosen house.

I don't look like an athlete anymore. I have a jaw disorder, I can't remember my own schedule, and I'm a disabled diabetic.

Head into the wall
> *Soccer ball to the face*
> *Knee to the head*
>> *Soccer ball to the head*
>>> *Elbow to the head*
>>> *Blow to the head*
>> *Collision with an open door*
>>> *Collision with a car door*
>> *Soft blow to the head*
> *Bicycle crash*
Volleyball to the head

I have trouble with cognition, and my migraines leave me crying in a dark room, overwhelmed by light, sound, and smell. I can't think. I can't think. I am meaner and sensitive.

I looked up the cost of epilepsy helmets once and whether they come in a fashionable variety (they do not). They're also expensive and bulky and invite too many questions. The science is certain—just don't get hit in the first place.

The folds of my brain will only show trauma when sliced thin. They will have to cut me open. It is "interesting," the research says. I am "interesting."

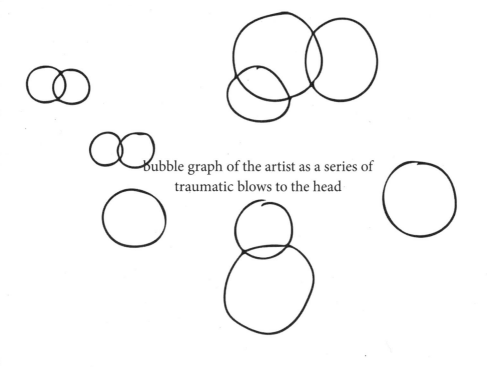

bubble graph of the artist as a series of
traumatic blows to the head

*A nurse at the University Health Clinic is convinced my boyfriend
is beating me (he isn't) because his fist connected with my head. It results
in a severe impairment for the next three months. The gauzy haze
returns. Concussions six through nine, arguments one to a hundred. The
doctor prescribes nortriptyline, an out-of-use antidepressant to combat
the screaming migraines that take over my brain every week. I am sick.
I fail my courses and withdraw, unable to access higher-level cognitive
functioning. So many words for my brain failing to get to work.*

there are no cures. short-term solutions are rest

long-term solutions are ????

where does that leave me? I have a heavy brain, a fragile living
thing that is trying so hard to keep itself alive. it is flawed. I have
not protected it as well as I could have. on Instagram, I chat with an
author who debuted a book of poetry, half of it written preconcussion,
and half written postconcussion. she told me of a new therapy for
people like her (because she does not know she is talking about people
like us). insurance will cover treatment if you are on government-
sanctioned long-term disability. I thought about how I am high
functioning and how disability funding is legislated poverty, putting
caps on the money you can earn. without it, the treatment is $20,000.
I didn't ask what it was.

I think if I had military dollars, what I'd do after ending the wars is to
cut open my own brain. the hungry scientists are as eager to get inside
it as I am to get out of it.

and when they'd spit me onto the sidewalk to be crushed beneath shoes,
I would ask:

reversible

compounding

decreasing with age

increasing with age

why I'm such an asshole

are the effects of my concussions   related to my mood disorder

related to my anxiety

preventable in the future

improvable with yoga

passable to my children

part of being disabled

forever?

Part 2: disease

you wouldn't like me when i'm angry
version 625.4 (N94.3)

untwist the ovaries, the burden of bearing fruit
the Naproxen works better than boiled ginger
there aren't enough bananas in the house
(after all, they are my father's favourite)
bleed through bedsheets and mattress
your favourite shorts
stop wearing white
wash in secret
can you fit your shame in the cabinet under the sink
do you carry extras for all the girls at school
hang the underwear on the curtain rod
don't ask why it hurts; don't tell anyone but your doctor
and if you're lucky, they might even believe you

Could you possibly have PMDD or PME?
Take this quiz!

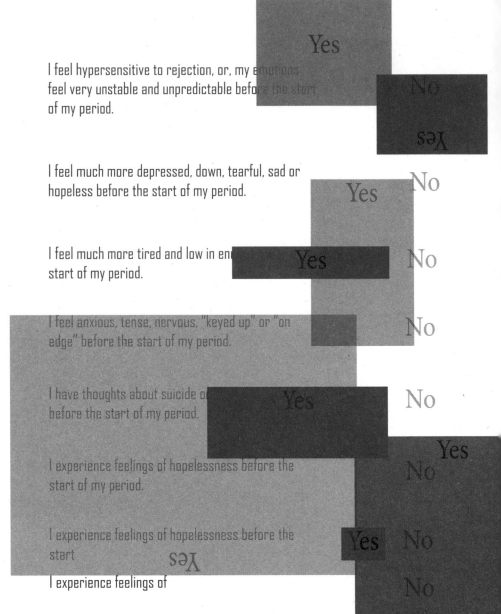

I feel hypersensitive to rejection, or, my emotions feel very unstable and unpredictable before the start of my period.

Yes   No

I feel much more depressed, down, tearful, sad or hopeless before the start of my period.

Yes   No

I feel much more tired and low in en... start of my period.

Yes   No

I feel anxious, tense, nervous, "keyed up" or "on edge" before the start of my period.

No

I have thoughts about suicide o... before the start of my period.

Yes   No

I experience feelings of hopelessness before the start of my period.

Yes   No

I experience feelings of hopelessness before the start

Yes   No

I experience feelings of

No

could you believe in a god that could forsake you for ten years?

~~the average woman will have 450 periods~~

██████████████████ ten ███ years.

███████ ██ good ████████ years.

████ sleep through the night, and ███ the toilet bowl, ███ wear the white underwear ██████████████████

█████████ be ██████ grateful for the ████████████████████ ██████████████████████████ thing that is killing me.

██████████████████

the average woman █████████████

▌could do so much ████████████

▌could be so good ████████████

▌could sleep through the night, and save the toilet bowl, and wear the white underwear every day. ███████████

I could have been more grateful for the ██████████████████ ████████████████████████ thing that is killing me.

████████████████████

██

██

████████████████████████████████████

███████████████████████████ save ████████████████
███████████████████████████████████

██
██████████████████████████████████ me.

████████████████████

Feelings of sadness and despair, even including suicidality, anxiety and panic attacks, crying, irritability and anger, lack of int
out of control are common. Assorted somatic symptoms include breast tenderness, bloating, headache and pain. Feelings of
and relationships, fatigue and tiredness, difficulty focusing or thinking, food cravings and binge eating, and feeling out of
including suicidality, anxiety and panic attacks, crying, irritability and anger, lack of interest in or attention to activities and r
somatic symptoms include breast tenderness, bloating, headache and pain. Feelings of sadness and despair, even including su
difficulty focusing or thinking, food cravings and binge eating, and feeling out of control are common. Assorted somatic
attacks, crying, irritability and anger, lack of interest in or attention to activities and relationships, fatigue and tiredness, di
tenderness, bloating, headache and pain. Feelings of sadness and despair, even including suicidality, anxiety and panic attac
food cravings and binge eating, and feeling out of control are common. Assorted somatic symptoms include breast tenderne
lack of interest in or attention to activities and relationships, fatigue and tiredness, difficulty focusing or thinking, food crav
Feelings of sadness and despair, even including suicidality, anxiety and panic attacks, crying, irritability and anger, lack of int
out of control are common. Assorted somatic symptoms include breast tenderness, bloating, headache and pain. Feelings of
and relationships, fatigue and tiredness, difficulty focusing or thinking, food cravings and binge eating, and feeling out of
including suicidality, anxiety and panic attacks, crying, irritability and anger, lack of interest in or attention to activities and r
somatic symptoms include breast tenderness, bloating, headache and pain. Feelings of sadness and despair, even including su
difficulty focusing or thinking, food cravings and binge eating, and feeling out of control are common. Assorted somatic
attacks, crying, irritability and anger, lack of interest in or attention to activities and relationships, fatigue and tiredness, di
tenderness, bloating, headache and pain. Feelings of sadness and despair, even including suicidality, anxiety and panic attac
food cravings and binge eating, and feeling out of control are common. Assorted somatic symptoms include breast tenderne
lack of interest in or attention to activities and relationships, fatigue and tiredness, difficulty focusing or thinking, food crav
Feelings of sadness and despair, even including suicidality, anxiety and panic attacks, crying, irritability and anger, lack of int
out of control are common. Assorted somatic symptoms include breast tenderness, bloating, headache and pain. Feelings of
and relationships, fatigue and tiredness, difficulty focusing or thinking, food cravings and binge eating, and feeling out of
including suicidality, anxiety and panic attacks, crying, irritability and anger, lack of interest in or attention to activities and r
somatic symptoms include breast tenderness, bloating, headache and pain. Feelings of sadness and despair, even including su
difficulty focusing or thinking, food cravings and binge eating, and feeling out of control are common. Assorted somatic
attacks, crying, irritability and anger, lack of interest in or attention to activities and relationships, fatigue and tiredness, di
tenderness, bloating, headache and pain. Feelings of sadness and despair, even including suicidality, anxiety and panic attac
food cravings and binge eating, and feeling out of control are common. Assorted somatic symptoms include breast tenderne
lack of interest in or attention to activities and relationships, fatigue and tiredness, difficulty focusing or thinking, food crav
Feelings of sadness and despair, even including suicidality, anxiety and panic attacks, crying, irritability and anger, lack of int
out of control are common. Assorted somatic symptoms include breast tenderness, bloating, headache and pain. Feelings of
and relationships, fatigue and tiredness, difficulty focusing or thinking, food cravings and binge eating, and feeling out of
including suicidality, anxiety and panic attacks, crying, irritability and anger, lack of interest in or attention to activities and r
somatic symptoms include breast tenderness, bloating, headache and pain. Feelings of sadness and despair, even including su
difficulty focusing or thinking, food cravings and binge eating, and feeling out of control are common. Assorted somatic
attacks, crying, irritability and anger, lack of interest in or attention to activities and relationships, fatigue and tiredness, di
tenderness, bloating, headache and pain. Feelings of sadness and despair, even including suicidality, anxiety and panic attac
food cravings and binge eating, and feeling out of control are common. Assorted somatic symptoms include breast tenderne
lack of interest in or attention to activities and relationships, fatigue and tiredness, difficulty focusing or thinking, food crav
Feelings of sadness and despair, even including suicidality, anxiety and panic attacks, crying, irritability and anger, lack of int
out of control are common. Assorted somatic symptoms include breast tenderness, bloating, headache and pain. Feelings of
and relationships, fatigue and tiredness, difficulty focusing or thinking, food cravings and binge eating, and feeling out of
including suicidality, anxiety and panic attacks, crying, irritability and anger, lack of interest in or attention to activities and r
somatic symptoms include breast tenderness, bloating, headache and pain. Feelings of sadness and despair, even including su
difficulty focusing or thinking, food cravings and binge eating, and feeling out of control are common. Assorted somatic
attacks, crying, irritability and anger, lack of interest in or attention to activities and relationships, fatigue and tiredness, di
tenderness, bloating, headache and pain. Feelings of sadness and despair, even including suicidality, anxiety and panic attac
food cravings and binge eating, and feeling out of control are common. Assorted somatic symptoms include breast tenderne
lack of interest in or attention to activities and relationships, fatigue and tiredness, difficulty focusing or thinking, food crav
Feelings of sadness and despair, even including suicidality, anxiety and panic attacks, crying, irritability and anger, lack of int
out of control are common. Assorted somatic symptoms include breast tenderness, bloating, headache and pain. Feelings of
and relationships, fatigue and tiredness, difficulty focusing or thinking, food cravings and binge eating, and feeling out of
including suicidality, anxiety and panic attacks, crying, irritability and anger, lack of interest in or attention to activities a

activities and relationships, fatigue and tiredness, difficulty focusing or thinking, food cravings and binge eating, and feeling
even including suicidality, anxiety and panic attacks, crying, irritability and anger, lack of interest in or attention to activities
Assorted somatic symptoms include breast tenderness, bloating, headache and pain. Feelings of sadness and despair, even
nd tiredness, difficulty focusing or thinking, food cravings and binge eating, and feeling out of control are common. Assorted
panic attacks, crying, irritability and anger, lack of interest in or attention to activities and relationships, fatigue and tiredness,
ast tenderness, bloating, headache and pain. Feelings of sadness and despair, even including suicidality, anxiety and panic
inking, food cravings and binge eating, and feeling out of control are common. Assorted somatic symptoms include breast
and anger, lack of interest in or attention to activities and relationships, fatigue and tiredness, difficulty focusing or thinking,
and pain. Feelings of sadness and despair, even including suicidality, anxiety and panic attacks, crying, irritability and anger,
and feeling out of control are common. Assorted somatic symptoms include breast tenderness, bloating, headache and pain.
activities and relationships, fatigue and tiredness, difficulty focusing or thinking, food cravings and binge eating, and feeling
even including suicidality, anxiety and panic attacks, crying, irritability and anger, lack of interest in or attention to activities
Assorted somatic symptoms include breast tenderness, bloating, headache and pain. Feelings of sadness and despair, even
nd tiredness, difficulty focusing or thinking, food cravings and binge eating, and feeling out of control are common. Assorted
panic attacks, crying, irritability and anger, lack of interest in or attention to activities and relationships, fatigue and tiredness,
ast tenderness, bloating, headache and pain. Feelings of sadness and despair, even including suicidality, anxiety and panic
inking, food cravings and binge eating, and feeling out of control are common. Assorted somatic symptoms include breast
and anger, lack of interest in or attention to activities and relationships, fatigue and tiredness, difficulty focusing or thinking,
and pain. Feelings of sadness and despair, even including suicidality, anxiety and panic attacks, crying, irritability and anger,
and feeling out of control are common. Assorted somatic symptoms include breast tenderness, bloating, headache and pain.
activities and relationships, fatigue and tiredness, difficulty focusing or thinking, food cravings and binge eating, and feeling
even including suicidality, anxiety and panic attacks, crying, irritability and anger, lack of interest in or attention to activities
Assorted somatic symptoms include breast tenderness, bloating, headache and pain. Feelings of sadness and despair, even
nd tiredness, difficulty focusing or thinking, food cravings and binge eating, and feeling out of control are common. Assorted
panic attacks, crying, irritability and anger, lack of interest in or attention to activities and relationships, fatigue and tiredness,
ast tenderness, bloating, headache and pain. Feelings of sadness and despair, even including suicidality, anxiety and panic
inking, food cravings and binge eating, and feeling out of control are common. Assorted somatic symptoms include breast
and anger, lack of interest in or attention to activities and relationships, fatigue and tiredness, difficulty focusing or thinking,
and pain. Feelings of sadness and despair, even including suicidality, anxiety and panic attacks, crying, irritability and anger,
and feeling out of control are common. Assorted somatic symptoms include breast tenderness, bloating, headache and pain.
activities and relationships, fatigue and tiredness, difficulty focusing or thinking, food cravings and binge eating, and feeling
even including suicidality, anxiety and panic attacks, crying, irritability and anger, lack of interest in or attention to activities
Assorted somatic symptoms include breast tenderness, bloating, headache and pain. Feelings of sadness and despair, even
nd tiredness, difficulty focusing or thinking, food cravings and binge eating, and feeling out of control are common. Assorted
panic attacks, crying, irritability and anger, lack of interest in or attention to activities and relationships, fatigue and tiredness,
ast tenderness, bloating, headache and pain. Feelings of sadness and despair, even including suicidality, anxiety and panic
inking, food cravings and binge eating, and feeling out of control are common. Assorted somatic symptoms include breast
and anger, lack of interest in or attention to activities and relationships, fatigue and tiredness, difficulty focusing or thinking,
and pain. Feelings of sadness and despair, even including suicidality, anxiety and panic attacks, crying, irritability and anger,
and feeling out of control are common. Assorted somatic symptoms include breast tenderness, bloating, headache and pain.
activities and relationships, fatigue and tiredness, difficulty focusing or thinking, food cravings and binge eating, and feeling
even including suicidality, anxiety and panic attacks, crying, irritability and anger, lack of interest in or attention to activities
Assorted somatic symptoms include breast tenderness, bloating, headache and pain. Feelings of sadness and despair, even
nd tiredness, difficulty focusing or thinking, food cravings and binge eating, and feeling out of control are common. Assorted
panic attacks, crying, irritability and anger, lack of interest in or attention to activities and relationships, fatigue and tiredness,
ast tenderness, bloating, headache and pain. Feelings of sadness and despair, even including suicidality, anxiety and panic
inking, food cravings and binge eating, and feeling out of control are common. Assorted somatic symptoms include breast
and anger, lack of interest in or attention to activities and relationships, fatigue and tiredness, difficulty focusing or thinking,
and pain. Feelings of sadness and despair, even including suicidality, anxiety and panic attacks, crying, irritability and anger,
and feeling out of control are common. Assorted somatic symptoms include breast tenderness, bloating, headache and pain.
activities and relationships, fatigue and tiredness, difficulty focusing or thinking, food cravings and binge eating, and feeling
even including suicidality, anxiety and panic attacks, crying, irritability and anger, lack of interest in or attention to activities
Assorted somatic symptoms include breast tenderness, bloating, headache and pain. Feelings of sadness and despair, even
gue and tiredness, difficulty focusing or thinking, food cravings and binge eating, and feeling out of control are common.

Feelings of sadness and despair, even including suicidality, anxiety and panic attacks, crying, irritability and anger, lack of int
out of control are common. Assorted somatic symptoms include breast tenderness, bloating, headache and pain. Feelings of
and relationships, fatigue and tiredness, difficulty focusing or thinking, food cravings and binge eating, and feeling out of
including suicidality, anxiety and panic attacks, crying, irritability and anger, lack of interest in or attention to activities and r
somatic symptoms include breast tenderness, bloating, headache and pain. Feelings of sadness and despair, even including su
difficulty focusing or thinking, food cravings and binge eating, and feeling out of control are common. Assorted somatic s
attacks, crying, irritability and anger, lack of interest in or attention to activities and relationships, fatigue and tiredness, di
tenderness, bloating, headache and pain. Feelings of sadness and despair, even including suicidality, anxiety and panic attac
food cravings and binge eating, and feeling out of control are common. Assorted somatic symptoms include breast tenderne
lack of interest in or attention to activities and relationships, fatigue and tiredness, difficulty focusing or thinking, food cravi
Feelings of sadness and despair, even including suicidality, anxiety and panic attacks, crying, irritability and anger, lack of int
out of control are common. Assorted somatic symptoms include breast tenderness, bloating, headache and pain. Feelings of
and relationships, fatigue and tiredness, difficulty focusing or thinking, food cravings and binge eating, and feeling out of
including suicidality, anxiety and panic attacks, crying, irritability and anger, lack of interest in or attention to activities and r
somatic symptoms include breast tenderness, bloating, headache and pain. Feelings of sadness and despair, even including su
difficulty focusing or thinking, food cravings and binge eating, and feeling out of control are common. Assorted somatic s
attacks, crying, irritability and anger, lack of interest in or attention to activities and relationships, fatigue and tiredness, di
tenderness, bloating, headache and pain. Feelings of sadness and despair, even including suicidality, anxiety and panic attac
food cravings and binge eating, and feeling out of control are common. Assorted somatic symptoms include breast tenderne
lack of interest in or attention to activities and relationships, fatigue and tiredness, difficulty focusing or thinking, food cravi
Feelings of sadness and despair, even including suicidality, anxiety and panic attacks, crying, irritability and anger, lack of int
out of control are common. Assorted somatic symptoms include breast tenderness, bloating, headache and pain. Feelings of
and relationships, fatigue and tiredness, difficulty focusing or thinking, food cravings and binge eating, and feeling out of
including suicidality, anxiety and panic attacks, crying, irritability and anger, lack of interest in or attention to activities and r
somatic symptoms include breast tenderness, bloating, headache and pain. Feelings of sadness and despair, even including su
difficulty focusing or thinking, food cravings and binge eating, and feeling out of control are common. Assorted somatic s
attacks, crying, irritability and anger, lack of interest in or attention to activities and relationships, fatigue and tiredness, di
tenderness, bloating, headache and pain. Feelings of sadness and despair, even including suicidality, anxiety and panic attac
food cravings and binge eating, and feeling out of control are common. Assorted somatic symptoms include breast tenderne
lack of interest in or attention to activities and relationships, fatigue and tiredness, difficulty focusing or thinking, food cravi
Feelings of sadness and despair, even including suicidality, anxiety and panic attacks, crying, irritability and anger, lack of int
out of control are common. Assorted somatic symptoms include breast tenderness, bloating, headache and pain. Feelings of
and relationships, fatigue and tiredness, difficulty focusing or thinking, food cravings and binge eating, and feeling out of
including suicidality, anxiety and panic attacks, crying, irritability and anger, lack of interest in or attention to activities and r
somatic symptoms include breast tenderness, bloating, headache and pain. Feelings of sadness and despair, even including su
difficulty focusing or thinking, food cravings and binge eating, and feeling out of control are common. Assorted somatic s
attacks, crying, irritability and anger, lack of interest in or attention to activities and relationships, fatigue and tiredness, di
tenderness, bloating, headache and pain. Feelings of sadness and despair, even including suicidality, anxiety and panic attac
food cravings and binge eating, and feeling out of control are common. Assorted somatic symptoms include breast tenderne
lack of interest in or attention to activities and relationships, fatigue and tiredness, difficulty focusing or thinking, food cravi
Feelings of sadness and despair, even including suicidality, anxiety and panic attacks, crying, irritability and anger, lack of int
out of control are common. Assorted somatic symptoms include breast tenderness, bloating, headache and pain. Feelings of
and relationships, fatigue and tiredness, difficulty focusing or thinking, food cravings and binge eating, and feeling out of
including suicidality, anxiety and panic attacks, crying, irritability and anger, lack of interest in or attention to activities and r
somatic symptoms include breast tenderness, bloating, headache and pain. Feelings of sadness and despair, even including su
difficulty focusing or thinking, food cravings and binge eating, and feeling out of control are common. Assorted somatic s
attacks, crying, irritability and anger, lack of interest in or attention to activities and relationships, fatigue and tiredness, di
tenderness, bloating, headache and pain. Feelings of sadness and despair, even including suicidality, anxiety and panic attac
food cravings and binge eating, and feeling out of control are common. Assorted somatic symptoms include breast tenderne
lack of interest in or attention to activities and relationships, fatigue and tiredness, difficulty focusing or thinking, food cravi
Feelings of sadness and despair, even including suicidality, anxiety and panic attacks, crying, irritability and anger, lack of int
out of control are common. Assorted somatic symptoms include breast tenderness, bloating, headache and pain. Feelings of
and relationships, fatigue and tiredness, difficulty focusing or thinking, food cravings and binge eating, and feeling out of
including suicidality, anxiety and panic attacks, crying, irritability and anger, lack of interest in or attention to activities and r
somatic symptoms include breast tenderness, bloating, headache and pain. Feelings of sadness and despair, even including su
difficulty focusing or thinking, food cravings and binge eating, and feeling out of control are common. Assorted somatic s
attacks, crying, irritability and anger, lack of interest in or attention to activities and relationships, fatigue and tiredness, di
tenderness, bloating, headache and pain. Feelings of sadness and despair, even including suicidality, anxiety and panic attac
food cravings and binge eating, and feeling out of control are common. Assorted somatic symptoms include breast tenderne
lack of interest in or attention to activities and relationships, fatigue and tiredness, difficulty focusing or thinking, food cravi
Feelings of sadness and despair, even including suicidality, anxiety and panic attacks, crying, irritability and anger, lack of int
out of control are common. Assorted somatic symptoms include breast tenderness, bloating, headache and pain. Feelings of
and relationships, fatigue and tiredness, difficulty focusing or thinking, food cravings and binge eating, and feeling out of
including suicidality, anxiety and panic attacks, crying, irritability and anger, lack of interest in or attention to activities a

o activities and relationships, fatigue and tiredness, difficulty focusing or thinking, food cravings and binge eating, and feeling
, even including suicidality, anxiety and panic attacks, crying, irritability and anger, lack of interest in or attention to activities
.. Assorted somatic symptoms include breast tenderness, bloating, headache and pain. Feelings of sadness and despair, even
and tiredness, difficulty focusing or thinking, food cravings and binge eating, and feeling out of control are common. Assorted
l panic attacks, crying, irritability and anger, lack of interest in or attention to activities and relationships, fatigue and tiredness,
-east tenderness, bloating, headache and pain. Feelings of sadness and despair, even including suicidality, anxiety and panic
-hinking, food cravings and binge eating, and feeling out of control are common. Assorted somatic symptoms include breast
- and anger, lack of interest in or attention to activities and relationships, fatigue and tiredness, difficulty focusing or thinking,
-e and pain. Feelings of sadness and despair, even including suicidality, anxiety and panic attacks, crying, irritability and anger,
-, and feeling out of control are common. Assorted somatic symptoms include breast tenderness, bloating, headache and pain.
o activities and relationships, fatigue and tiredness, difficulty focusing or thinking, food cravings and binge eating, and feeling
, even including suicidality, anxiety and panic attacks, crying, irritability and anger, lack of interest in or attention to activities
.. Assorted somatic symptoms include breast tenderness, bloating, headache and pain. Feelings of sadness and despair, even
and tiredness, difficulty focusing or thinking, food cravings and binge eating, and feeling out of control are common. Assorted
l panic attacks, crying, irritability and anger, lack of interest in or attention to activities and relationships, fatigue and tiredness,
-east tenderness, bloating, headache and pain. Feelings of sadness and despair, even including suicidality, anxiety and panic
-hinking, food cravings and binge eating, and feeling out of control are common. Assorted somatic symptoms include breast
- and anger, lack of interest in or attention to activities and relationships, fatigue and tiredness, difficulty focusing or thinking,
-e and pain. Feelings of sadness and despair, even including suicidality, anxiety and panic attacks, crying, irritability and anger,
-, and feeling out of control are common. Assorted somatic symptoms include breast tenderness, bloating, headache and pain.
o activities and relationships, fatigue and tiredness, difficulty focusing or thinking, food cravings and binge eating, and feeling
, even including suicidality, anxiety and panic attacks, crying, irritability and anger, lack of interest in or attention to activities
.. Assorted somatic symptoms include breast tenderness, bloating, headache and pain. Feelings of sadness and despair, even
and tiredness, difficulty focusing or thinking, food cravings and binge eating, and feeling out of control are common. Assorted
l panic attacks, crying, irritability and anger, lack of interest in or attention to activities and relationships, fatigue and tiredness,
-east tenderness, bloating, headache and pain. Feelings of sadness and despair, even including suicidality, anxiety and panic
-hinking, food cravings and binge eating, and feeling out of control are common. Assorted somatic symptoms include breast
- and anger, lack of interest in or attention to activities and relationships, fatigue and tiredness, difficulty focusing or thinking,
-e and pain. Feelings of sadness and despair, even including suicidality, anxiety and panic attacks, crying, irritability and anger,
-, and feeling out of control are common. Assorted somatic symptoms include breast tenderness, bloating, headache and pain.
o activities and relationships, fatigue and tiredness, difficulty focusing or thinking, food cravings and binge eating, and feeling
, even including suicidality, anxiety and panic attacks, crying, irritability and anger, lack of interest in or attention to activities
.. Assorted somatic symptoms include breast tenderness, bloating, headache and pain. Feelings of sadness and despair, even
and tiredness, difficulty focusing or thinking, food cravings and binge eating, and feeling out of control are common. Assorted
l panic attacks, crying, irritability and anger, lack of interest in or attention to activities and relationships, fatigue and tiredness,
-east tenderness, bloating, headache and pain. Feelings of sadness and despair, even including suicidality, anxiety and panic
-hinking, food cravings and binge eating, and feeling out of control are common. Assorted somatic symptoms include breast
- and anger, lack of interest in or attention to activities and relationships, fatigue and tiredness, difficulty focusing or thinking,
-e and pain. Feelings of sadness and despair, even including suicidality, anxiety and panic attacks, crying, irritability and anger,
-, and feeling out of control are common. Assorted somatic symptoms include breast tenderness, bloating, headache and pain.
o activities and relationships, fatigue and tiredness, difficulty focusing or thinking, food cravings and binge eating, and feeling
, even including suicidality, anxiety and panic attacks, crying, irritability and anger, lack of interest in or attention to activities.
.. Assorted somatic symptoms include breast tenderness, bloating, headache and pain. Feelings of sadness and despair, even
and tiredness, difficulty focusing or thinking, food cravings and binge eating, and feeling out of control are common. Assorted
l panic attacks, crying, irritability and anger, lack of interest in or attention to activities and relationships, fatigue and tiredness,
-east tenderness, bloating, headache and pain. Feelings of sadness and despair, even including suicidality, anxiety and panic
-hinking, food cravings and binge eating, and feeling out of control are common. Assorted somatic symptoms include breast
- and anger, lack of interest in or attention to activities and relationships, fatigue and tiredness, difficulty focusing or thinking,
-e and pain. Feelings of sadness and despair, even including suicidality, anxiety and panic attacks, crying, irritability and anger,
-, and feeling out of control are common. Assorted somatic symptoms include breast tenderness, bloating, headache and pain.
o activities and relationships, fatigue and tiredness, difficulty focusing or thinking, food cravings and binge eating, and feeling
, even including suicidality, anxiety and panic attacks, crying, irritability and anger, lack of interest in or attention to activities
.. Assorted somatic symptoms include breast tenderness, bloating, headache and pain. Feelings of sadness and despair, even
and tiredness, difficulty focusing or thinking, food cravings and binge eating, and feeling out of control are common. Assorted
l panic attacks, crying, irritability and anger, lack of interest in or attention to activities and relationships, fatigue and tiredness,
-east tenderness, bloating, headache and pain. Feelings of sadness and despair, even including suicidality, anxiety and panic
-hinking, food cravings and binge eating, and feeling out of control are common. Assorted somatic symptoms include breast
- and anger, lack of interest in or attention to activities and relationships, fatigue and tiredness, difficulty focusing or thinking,
-e and pain. Feelings of sadness and despair, even including suicidality, anxiety and panic attacks, crying, irritability and anger,
-, and feeling out of control are common. Assorted somatic symptoms include breast tenderness, bloating, headache and pain.
o activities and relationships, fatigue and tiredness, difficulty focusing or thinking, food cravings and binge eating, and feeling
, even including suicidality, anxiety and panic attacks, crying, irritability and anger, lack of interest in or attention to activities
.. Assorted somatic symptoms include breast tenderness, bloating, headache and pain. Feelings of sadness and despair, even
igue and tiredness, difficulty focusing or thinking, food cravings and binge eating, and feeling out of control are common.

Feelings of sadness and despair, even including suicidality, anxiety and panic attacks, crying, irritability and anger, lack of inte
out of control are common. Assorted somatic symptoms include breast tenderness, bloating, headache and pain. Feelings of s
and relationships, fatigue and tiredness, difficulty focusing or thinking, food cravings and binge eating, and feeling out of c
including suicidality, anxiety and panic attacks, crying, irritability and anger, lack of interest in or attention to activities and rel
somatic symptoms include breast tenderness, bloating, headache and pain. Feelings of sadness and despair, even including sui
difficulty focusing or thinking, food cravings and binge eating, and feeling out of control are common. Assorted somatic sy
attacks, crying, irritability and anger, lack of interest in or attention to activities and relationships, fatigue and tiredness, diff
tenderness, bloating, headache and pain. Feelings of sadness and despair, even including suicidality, anxiety and panic attacks
food cravings and binge eating, and feeling out of control are common. Assorted somatic symptoms include breast tenderness
lack of interest in or attention to activities and relationships, fatigue and tiredness, difficulty focusing or thinking, food cravin
Feelings of sadness and despair, even including suicidality, anxiety and panic attacks, crying, irritability and anger, lack of inte
out of control are common. Assorted somatic symptoms include breast tenderness, bloating, headache and pain. Feelings of s
and relationships, fatigue and tiredness, difficulty focusing or thinking, food cravings and binge eating, and feeling out of c
including suicidality, anxiety and panic attacks, crying, irritability and anger, lack of interest in or attention to activities and rel
somatic symptoms include breast tenderness, bloating, headache and pain. Feelings of sadness and despair, even including sui
difficulty focusing or thinking, food cravings and binge eating, and feeling out of control are common. Assorted somatic sy
attacks, crying, irritability and anger, lack of interest in or attention to activities and relationships, fatigue and tiredness, diff
tenderness, bloating, headache and pain. Feelings of sadness and despair, even including suicidality, anxiety and panic attacks
food cravings and binge eating, and feeling out of control are common. Assorted somatic symptoms include breast tenderness
lack of interest in or attention to activities and relationships, fatigue and tiredness, difficulty focusing or thinking, food cravin
Feelings of sadness and despair, even including suicidality, anxiety and panic attacks, crying, irritability and anger, lack of inte
out of control are common. Assorted somatic symptoms include breast tenderness, bloating, headache and pain. Feelings of s
and relationships, fatigue and tiredness, difficulty focusing or thinking, food cravings and binge eating, and feeling out of c
including suicidality, anxiety and panic attacks, crying, irritability and anger, lack of interest in or attention to activities and rel
somatic symptoms include breast tenderness, bloating, headache and pain. Feelings of sadness and despair, even including sui
difficulty focusing or thinking, food cravings and binge eating, and feeling out of control are common. Assorted somatic sy
attacks, crying, irritability and anger, lack of interest in or attention to activities and relationships, fatigue and tiredness, diff
tenderness, bloating, headache and pain. Feelings of sadness and despair, even including suicidality, anxiety and panic attacks
food cravings and binge eating, and feeling out of control are common. Assorted somatic symptoms include breast tenderness
lack of interest in or attention to activities and relationships, fatigue and tiredness, difficulty focusing or thinking, food cravin
Feelings of sadness and despair, even including suicidality, anxiety and panic attacks, crying, irritability and anger, lack of inte
out of control are common. Assorted somatic symptoms include breast tenderness, bloating, headache and pain. Feelings of s
and relationships, fatigue and tiredness, difficulty focusing or thinking, food cravings and binge eating, and feeling out of c
including suicidality, anxiety and panic attacks, crying, irritability and anger, lack of interest in or attention to activities and rel
somatic symptoms include breast tenderness, bloating, headache and pain. Feelings of sadness and despair, even including sui
difficulty focusing or thinking, food cravings and binge eating, and feeling out of control are common. Assorted somatic sy
attacks, crying, irritability and anger, lack of interest in or attention to activities and relationships, fatigue and tiredness, diff
tenderness, bloating, headache and pain. Feelings of sadness and despair, even including suicidality, anxiety and panic attacks
food cravings and binge eating, and feeling out of control are common. Assorted somatic symptoms include breast tenderness
lack of interest in or attention to activities and relationships, fatigue and tiredness, difficulty focusing or thinking, food cravin
Feelings of sadness and despair, even including suicidality, anxiety and panic attacks, crying, irritability and anger, lack of inte
out of control are common. Assorted somatic symptoms include breast tenderness, bloating, headache and pain. Feelings of s
and relationships, fatigue and tiredness, difficulty focusing or thinking, food cravings and binge eating, and feeling out of c
including suicidality, anxiety and panic attacks, crying, irritability and anger, lack of interest in or attention to activities and rel
somatic symptoms include breast tenderness, bloating, headache and pain. Feelings of sadness and despair, even including sui
difficulty focusing or thinking, food cravings and binge eating, and feeling out of control are common. Assorted somatic sy
attacks, crying, irritability and anger, lack of interest in or attention to activities and relationships, fatigue and tiredness, diff
tenderness, bloating, headache and pain. Feelings of sadness and despair, even including suicidality, anxiety and panic attacks
food cravings and binge eating, and feeling out of control are common. Assorted somatic symptoms include breast tenderness
lack of interest in or attention to activities and relationships, fatigue and tiredness, difficulty focusing or thinking, food cravin
Feelings of sadness and despair, even including suicidality, anxiety and panic attacks, crying, irritability and anger, lack of inte
out of control are common. Assorted somatic symptoms include breast tenderness, bloating, headache and pain. Feelings of s
and relationships, fatigue and tiredness, difficulty focusing or thinking, food cravings and binge eating, and feeling out of c
including suicidality, anxiety and panic attacks, crying, irritability and anger, lack of interest in or attention to activities and rel
somatic symptoms include breast tenderness, bloating, headache and pain. Feelings of sadness and despair, even including sui
difficulty focusing or thinking, food cravings and binge eating, and feeling out of control are common. Assorted somatic sy
attacks, crying, irritability and anger, lack of interest in or attention to activities and relationships, fatigue and tiredness, diff
tenderness, bloating, headache and pain. Feelings of sadness and despair, even including suicidality, anxiety and panic attacks
food cravings and binge eating, and feeling out of control are common. Assorted somatic symptoms include breast tenderness
lack of interest in or attention to activities and relationships, fatigue and tiredness, difficulty focusing or thinking, food cravin
Feelings of sadness and despair, even including suicidality, anxiety and panic attacks, crying, irritability and anger, lack of inte
out of control are common. Assorted somatic symptoms include breast tenderness, bloating, headache and pain. Feelings of s
and relationships, fatigue and tiredness, difficulty focusing or thinking, food cravings and binge eating, and feeling out of c
including suicidality, anxiety and panic attacks, crying, irritability and anger, lack of interest in or attention to activities an

o activities and relationships, fatigue and tiredness, difficulty focusing or thinking, food cravings and binge eating, and feeling
, even including suicidality, anxiety and panic attacks, crying, irritability and anger, lack of interest in or attention to activities
. Assorted somatic symptoms include breast tenderness, bloating, headache and pain. Feelings of sadness and despair, even
and tiredness, difficulty focusing or thinking, food cravings and binge eating, and feeling out of control are common. Assorted
panic attacks, crying, irritability and anger, lack of interest in or attention to activities and relationships, fatigue and tiredness,
east tenderness, bloating, headache and pain. Feelings of sadness and despair, even including suicidality, anxiety and panic
hinking, food cravings and binge eating, and feeling out of control are common. Assorted somatic symptoms include breast
and anger, lack of interest in or attention to activities and relationships, fatigue and tiredness, difficulty focusing or thinking,
e and pain. Feelings of sadness and despair, even including suicidality, anxiety and panic attacks, crying, irritability and anger,
, and feeling out of control are common. Assorted somatic symptoms include breast tenderness, bloating, headache and pain.
o activities and relationships, fatigue and tiredness, difficulty focusing or thinking, food cravings and binge eating, and feeling
, even including suicidality, anxiety and panic attacks, crying, irritability and anger, lack of interest in or attention to activities
. Assorted somatic symptoms include breast tenderness, bloating, headache and pain. Feelings of sadness and despair, even
and tiredness, difficulty focusing or thinking, food cravings and binge eating, and feeling out of control are common. Assorted
panic attacks, crying, irritability and anger, lack of interest in or attention to activities and relationships, fatigue and tiredness,
east tenderness, bloating, headache and pain. Feelings of sadness and despair, even including suicidality, anxiety and panic
hinking, food cravings and binge eating, and feeling out of control are common. Assorted somatic symptoms include breast
and anger, lack of interest in or attention to activities and relationships, fatigue and tiredness, difficulty focusing or thinking,
e and pain. Feelings of sadness and despair, even including suicidality, anxiety and panic attacks, crying, irritability and anger,
, and feeling out of control are common. Assorted somatic symptoms include breast tenderness, bloating, headache and pain.
o activities and relationships, fatigue and tiredness, difficulty focusing or thinking, food cravings and binge eating, and feeling
, even including suicidality, anxiety and panic attacks, crying, irritability and anger, lack of interest in or attention to activities
. Assorted somatic symptoms include breast tenderness, bloating, headache and pain. Feelings of sadness and despair, even
and tiredness, difficulty focusing or thinking, food cravings and binge eating, and feeling out of control are common. Assorted
panic attacks, crying, irritability and anger, lack of interest in or attention to activities and relationships, fatigue and tiredness,
east tenderness, bloating, headache and pain. Feelings of sadness and despair, even including suicidality, anxiety and panic
hinking, food cravings and binge eating, and feeling out of control are common. Assorted somatic symptoms include breast
and anger, lack of interest in or attention to activities and relationships, fatigue and tiredness, difficulty focusing or thinking,
e and pain. Feelings of sadness and despair, even including suicidality, anxiety and panic attacks, crying, irritability and anger,
, and feeling out of control are common. Assorted somatic symptoms include breast tenderness, bloating, headache and pain.
o activities and relationships, fatigue and tiredness, difficulty focusing or thinking, food cravings and binge eating, and feeling
, even including suicidality, anxiety and panic attacks, crying, irritability and anger, lack of interest in or attention to activities
. Assorted somatic symptoms include breast tenderness, bloating, headache and pain. Feelings of sadness and despair, even
and tiredness, difficulty focusing or thinking, food cravings and binge eating, and feeling out of control are common. Assorted
panic attacks, crying, irritability and anger, lack of interest in or attention to activities and relationships, fatigue and tiredness,
east tenderness, bloating, headache and pain. Feelings of sadness and despair, even including suicidality, anxiety and panic
hinking, food cravings and binge eating, and feeling out of control are common. Assorted somatic symptoms include breast
and anger, lack of interest in or attention to activities and relationships, fatigue and tiredness, difficulty focusing or thinking,
e and pain. Feelings of sadness and despair, even including suicidality, anxiety and panic attacks, crying, irritability and anger,
, and feeling out of control are common. Assorted somatic symptoms include breast tenderness, bloating, headache and pain.
o activities and relationships, fatigue and tiredness, difficulty focusing or thinking, food cravings and binge eating, and feeling
, even including suicidality, anxiety and panic attacks, crying, irritability and anger, lack of interest in or attention to activities
. Assorted somatic symptoms include breast tenderness, bloating, headache and pain. Feelings of sadness and despair, even
and tiredness, difficulty focusing or thinking, food cravings and binge eating, and feeling out of control are common. Assorted
panic attacks, crying, irritability and anger, lack of interest in or attention to activities and relationships, fatigue and tiredness,
east tenderness, bloating, headache and pain. Feelings of sadness and despair, even including suicidality, anxiety and panic
hinking, food cravings and binge eating, and feeling out of control are common. Assorted somatic symptoms include breast
and anger, lack of interest in or attention to activities and relationships, fatigue and tiredness, difficulty focusing or thinking,
e and pain. Feelings of sadness and despair, even including suicidality, anxiety and panic attacks, crying, irritability and anger,
, and feeling out of control are common. Assorted somatic symptoms include breast tenderness, bloating, headache and pain.
o activities and relationships, fatigue and tiredness, difficulty focusing or thinking, food cravings and binge eating, and feeling
, even including suicidality, anxiety and panic attacks, crying, irritability and anger, lack of interest in or attention to activities
. Assorted somatic symptoms include breast tenderness, bloating, headache and pain. Feelings of sadness and despair, even
igue and tiredness, difficulty focusing or thinking, food cravings and binge eating, and feeling out of control are common.

Feelings of sadness and despair, even including suicidality, anxiety and panic attacks, crying, irritability and anger, lack of inte
out of control are common. Assorted somatic symptoms include breast tenderness, bloating, headache and pain. Feelings of s
and relationships, fatigue and tiredness, difficulty focusing or thinking, food cravings and binge eating, and feeling out of c
including suicidality, anxiety and panic attacks, crying, irritability and anger, lack of interest in or attention to activities and re
somatic symptoms include breast tenderness, bloating, headache and pain. Feelings of sadness and despair, even including sui
difficulty focusing or thinking, food cravings and binge eating, and feeling out of control are common. Assorted somatic sy
attacks, crying, irritability and anger, lack of interest in or attention to activities and relationships, fatigue and tiredness, dif
tenderness, bloating, headache and pain. Feelings of sadness and despair, even including suicidality, anxiety and panic attack
food cravings and binge eating, and feeling out of control are common. Assorted somatic symptoms include breast tenderness
lack of interest in or attention to activities and relationships, fatigue and tiredness, difficulty focusing or thinking, food cravir
Feelings of sadness and despair, even including suicidality, anxiety and panic attacks, crying, irritability and anger, lack of inte
out of control are common. Assorted somatic symptoms include breast tenderness, bloating, headache and pain. Feelings of s
and relationships, fatigue and tiredness, difficulty focusing or thinking, food cravings and binge eating, and feeling out of c
including suicidality, anxiety and panic attacks, crying, irritability and anger, lack of interest in or attention to activities and re
somatic symptoms include breast tenderness, bloating, headache and pain. Feelings of sadness and despair, even including sui
difficulty focusing or thinking, food cravings and binge eating, and feeling out of control are common. Assorted somatic sy
attacks, crying, irritability and anger, lack of interest in or attention to activities and relationships, fatigue and tiredness, dif
tenderness, bloating, headache and pain. Feelings of sadness and despair, even including suicidality, anxiety and panic attack
food cravings and binge eating, and feeling out of control are common. Assorted somatic symptoms include breast tenderness
lack of interest in or attention to activities and relationships, fatigue and tiredness, difficulty focusing or thinking, food cravir
Feelings of sadness and despair, even including suicidality, anxiety and panic attacks, crying, irritability and anger, lack of inte
out of control are common. Assorted somatic symptoms include breast tenderness, bloating, headache and pain. Feelings of s
and relationships, fatigue and tiredness, difficulty focusing or thinking, food cravings and binge eating, and feeling out of c
including suicidality, anxiety and panic attacks, crying, irritability and anger, lack of interest in or attention to activities and re
somatic symptoms include breast tenderness, bloating, headache and pain. Feelings of sadness and despair, even including sui
difficulty focusing or thinking, food cravings and binge eating, and feeling out of control are common. Assorted somatic sy
attacks, crying, irritability and anger, lack of interest in or attention to activities and relationships, fatigue and tiredness, dif
tenderness, bloating, headache and pain. Feelings of sadness and despair, even including suicidality, anxiety and panic attack
food cravings and binge eating, and feeling out of control are common. Assorted somatic symptoms include breast tenderness
lack of interest in or attention to activities and relationships, fatigue and tiredness, difficulty focusing or thinking, food cravir
Feelings of sadness and despair, even including suicidality, anxiety and panic attacks, crying, irritability and anger, lack of inte
out of control are common. Assorted somatic symptoms include breast tenderness, bloating, headache and pain. Feelings of s
and relationships, fatigue and tiredness, difficulty focusing or thinking, food cravings and binge eating, and feeling out of c
including suicidality, anxiety and panic attacks, crying, irritability and anger, lack of interest in or attention to activities and re
somatic symptoms include breast tenderness, bloating, headache and pain. Feelings of sadness and despair, even including sui
difficulty focusing or thinking, food cravings and binge eating, and feeling out of control are common. Assorted somatic sy
attacks, crying, irritability and anger, lack of interest in or attention to activities and relationships, fatigue and tiredness, dif
tenderness, bloating, headache and pain. Feelings of sadness and despair, even including suicidality, anxiety and panic attack
food cravings and binge eating, and feeling out of control are common. Assorted somatic symptoms include breast tenderness
lack of interest in or attention to activities and relationships, fatigue and tiredness, difficulty focusing or thinking, food cravir
Feelings of sadness and despair, even including suicidality, anxiety and panic attacks, crying, irritability and anger, lack of inte
out of control are common. Assorted somatic symptoms include breast tenderness, bloating, headache and pain. Feelings of s
and relationships, fatigue and tiredness, difficulty focusing or thinking, food cravings and binge eating, and feeling out of c
including suicidality, anxiety and panic attacks, crying, irritability and anger, lack of interest in or attention to activities and re
somatic symptoms include breast tenderness, bloating, headache and pain. Feelings of sadness and despair, even including sui
difficulty focusing or thinking, food cravings and binge eating, and feeling out of control are common. Assorted somatic sy
attacks, crying, irritability and anger, lack of interest in or attention to activities and relationships, fatigue and tiredness, dif
tenderness, bloating, headache and pain. Feelings of sadness and despair, even including suicidality, anxiety and panic attack
food cravings and binge eating, and feeling out of control are common. Assorted somatic symptoms include breast tenderness
lack of interest in or attention to activities and relationships, fatigue and tiredness, difficulty focusing or thinking, food cravir
Feelings of sadness and despair, even including suicidality, anxiety and panic attacks, crying, irritability and anger, lack of inte
out of control are common. Assorted somatic symptoms include breast tenderness, bloating, headache and pain. Feelings of s
and relationships, fatigue and tiredness, difficulty focusing or thinking, food cravings and binge eating, and feeling out of c
including suicidality, anxiety and panic attacks, crying, irritability and anger, lack of interest in or attention to activities and re
somatic symptoms include breast tenderness, bloating, headache and pain. Feelings of sadness and despair, even including sui
difficulty focusing or thinking, food cravings and binge eating, and feeling out of control are common. Assorted somatic sy
attacks, crying, irritability and anger, lack of interest in or attention to activities and relationships, fatigue and tiredness, dif
tenderness, bloating, headache and pain. Feelings of sadness and despair, even including suicidality, anxiety and panic attack
food cravings and binge eating, and feeling out of control are common. Assorted somatic symptoms include breast tenderness
lack of interest in or attention to activities and relationships, fatigue and tiredness, difficulty focusing or thinking, food cravir
Feelings of sadness and despair, even including suicidality, anxiety and panic attacks, crying, irritability and anger, lack of inte
out of control are common. Assorted somatic symptoms include breast tenderness, bloating, headache and pain. Feelings of s
and relationships, fatigue and tiredness, difficulty focusing or thinking, food cravings and binge eating, and feeling out of c
including suicidality, anxiety and panic attacks, crying, irritability and anger, lack of interest in or attention to activities ar

activities and relationships, fatigue and tiredness, difficulty focusing or thinking, food cravings and binge eating, and feeling even including suicidality, anxiety and panic attacks, crying, irritability and anger, lack of interest in or attention to activities Assorted somatic symptoms include breast tenderness, bloating, headache and pain. Feelings of sadness and despair, even nd tiredness, difficulty focusing or thinking, food cravings and binge eating, and feeling out of control are common. Assorted panic attacks, crying, irritability and anger, lack of interest in or attention to activities and relationships, fatigue and tiredness, ast tenderness, bloating, headache and pain. Feelings of sadness and despair, even including suicidality, anxiety and panic inking, food cravings and binge eating, and feeling out of control are common. Assorted somatic symptoms include breast and anger, lack of interest in or attention to activities and relationships, fatigue and tiredness, difficulty focusing or thinking, and pain. Feelings of sadness and despair, even including suicidality, anxiety and panic attacks, crying, irritability and anger, and feeling out of control are common. Assorted somatic symptoms include breast tenderness, bloating, headache and pain. activities and relationships, fatigue and tiredness, difficulty focusing or thinking, food cravings and binge eating, and feeling even including suicidality, anxiety and panic attacks, crying, irritability and anger, lack of interest in or attention to activities Assorted somatic symptoms include breast tenderness, bloating, headache and pain. Feelings of sadness and despair, even nd tiredness, difficulty focusing or thinking, food cravings and binge eating, and feeling out of control are common. Assorted panic attacks, crying, irritability and anger, lack of interest in or attention to activities and relationships, fatigue and tiredness, ast tenderness, bloating, headache and pain. Feelings of sadness and despair, even including suicidality, anxiety and panic inking, food cravings and binge eating, and feeling out of control are common. Assorted somatic symptoms include breast and anger, lack of interest in or attention to activities and relationships, fatigue and tiredness, difficulty focusing or thinking, and pain. Feelings of sadness and despair, even including suicidality, anxiety and panic attacks, crying, irritability and anger, and feeling out of control are common. Assorted somatic symptoms include breast tenderness, bloating, headache and pain. activities and relationships, fatigue and tiredness, difficulty focusing or thinking, food cravings and binge eating, and feeling even including suicidality, anxiety and panic attacks, crying, irritability and anger, lack of interest in or attention to activities Assorted somatic symptoms include breast tenderness, bloating, headache and pain. Feelings of sadness and despair, even nd tiredness, difficulty focusing or thinking, food cravings and binge eating, and feeling out of control are common. Assorted panic attacks, crying, irritability and anger, lack of interest in or attention to activities and relationships, fatigue and tiredness, ast tenderness, bloating, headache and pain. Feelings of sadness and despair, even including suicidality, anxiety and panic inking, food cravings and binge eating, and feeling out of control are common. Assorted somatic symptoms include breast and anger, lack of interest in or attention to activities and relationships, fatigue and tiredness, difficulty focusing or thinking, and pain. Feelings of sadness and despair, even including suicidality, anxiety and panic attacks, crying, irritability and anger, and feeling out of control are common. Assorted somatic symptoms include breast tenderness, bloating, headache and pain. activities and relationships, fatigue and tiredness, difficulty focusing or thinking, food cravings and binge eating, and feeling even including suicidality, anxiety and panic attacks, crying, irritability and anger, lack of interest in or attention to activities Assorted somatic symptoms include breast tenderness, bloating, headache and pain. Feelings of sadness and despair, even nd tiredness, difficulty focusing or thinking, food cravings and binge eating, and feeling out of control are common. Assorted panic attacks, crying, irritability and anger, lack of interest in or attention to activities and relationships, fatigue and tiredness, ast tenderness, bloating, headache and pain. Feelings of sadness and despair, even including suicidality, anxiety and panic inking, food cravings and binge eating, and feeling out of control are common. Assorted somatic symptoms include breast and anger, lack of interest in or attention to activities and relationships, fatigue and tiredness, difficulty focusing or thinking, and pain. Feelings of sadness and despair, even including suicidality, anxiety and panic attacks, crying, irritability and anger, and feeling out of control are common. Assorted somatic symptoms include breast tenderness, bloating, headache and pain. activities and relationships, fatigue and tiredness, difficulty focusing or thinking, food cravings and binge eating, and feeling even including suicidality, anxiety and panic attacks, crying, irritability and anger, lack of interest in or attention to activities Assorted somatic symptoms include breast tenderness, bloating, headache and pain. Feelings of sadness and despair, even nd tiredness, difficulty focusing or thinking, food cravings and binge eating, and feeling out of control are common. Assorted panic attacks, crying, irritability and anger, lack of interest in or attention to activities and relationships, fatigue and tiredness, ast tenderness, bloating, headache and pain. Feelings of sadness and despair, even including suicidality, anxiety and panic inking, food cravings and binge eating, and feeling out of control are common. Assorted somatic symptoms include breast and anger, lack of interest in or attention to activities and relationships, fatigue and tiredness, difficulty focusing or thinking, and pain. Feelings of sadness and despair, even including suicidality, anxiety and panic attacks, crying, irritability and anger, and feeling out of control are common. Assorted somatic symptoms include breast tenderness, bloating, headache and pain. activities and relationships, fatigue and tiredness, difficulty focusing or thinking, food cravings and binge eating, and feeling even including suicidality, anxiety and panic attacks, crying, irritability and anger, lack of interest in or attention to activities Assorted somatic symptoms include breast tenderness, bloating, headache and pain. Feelings of sadness and despair, even gue and tiredness, difficulty focusing or thinking, food cravings and binge eating, and feeling out of control are common.

Feelings of sadness and despair, even including suicidality, anxiety and panic attacks, crying, irritability and anger, lack of inte
out of control are common. Assorted somatic symptoms include breast tenderness, bloating, headache and pain. Feelings of
and relationships, fatigue and tiredness, difficulty focusing or thinking, food cravings and binge eating, and feeling out of
including suicidality, anxiety and panic attacks, crying, irritability and anger, lack of interest in or attention to activities and re
somatic symptoms include breast tenderness, bloating, headache and pain. Feelings of sadness and despair, even including su
difficulty focusing or thinking, food cravings and binge eating, and feeling out of control are common. Assorted somatic s
attacks, crying, irritability and anger, lack of interest in or attention to activities and relationships, fatigue and tiredness, di
tenderness, bloating, headache and pain. Feelings of sadness and despair, even including suicidality, anxiety and panic attac
food cravings and binge eating, and feeling out of control are common. Assorted somatic symptoms include breast tenderne
lack of interest in or attention to activities and relationships, fatigue and tiredness, difficulty focusing or thinking, food cravi
Feelings of sadness and despair, even including suicidality, anxiety and panic attacks, crying, irritability and anger, lack of inte
out of control are common. Assorted somatic symptoms include breast tenderness, bloating, headache and pain. Feelings of
and relationships, fatigue and tiredness, difficulty focusing or thinking, food cravings and binge eating, and feeling out of
including suicidality, anxiety and panic attacks, crying, irritability and anger, lack of interest in or attention to activities and re
somatic symptoms include breast tenderness, bloating, headache and pain. Feelings of sadness and despair, even including su
difficulty focusing or thinking, food cravings and binge eating, and feeling out of control are common. Assorted somatic s
attacks, crying, irritability and anger, lack of interest in or attention to activities and relationships, fatigue and tiredness, di
tenderness, bloating, headache and pain. Feelings of sadness and despair, even including suicidality, anxiety and panic attac
food cravings and binge eating, and feeling out of control are common. Assorted somatic symptoms include breast tenderne
lack of interest in or attention to activities and relationships, fatigue and tiredness, difficulty focusing or thinking, food cravi
Feelings of sadness and despair, even including suicidality, anxiety and panic attacks, crying, irritability and anger, lack of int
out of control are common. Assorted somatic symptoms include breast tenderness, bloating, headache and pain. Feelings of
and relationships, fatigue and tiredness, difficulty focusing or thinking, food cravings and binge eating, and feeling out of
including suicidality, anxiety and panic attacks, crying, irritability and anger, lack of interest in or attention to activities and r
somatic symptoms include breast tenderness, bloating, headache and pain. Feelings of sadness and despair, even including su
difficulty focusing or thinking, food cravings and binge eating, and feeling out of control are common. Assorted somatic s
attacks, crying, irritability and anger, lack of interest in or attention to activities and relationships, fatigue and tiredness, di
tenderness, bloating, headache and pain. Feelings of sadness and despair, even including suicidality, anxiety and panic attac
food cravings and binge eating, and feeling out of control are common. Assorted somatic symptoms include breast tenderne
lack of interest in or attention to activities and relationships, fatigue and tiredness, difficulty focusing or thinking, food cravi
Feelings of sadness and despair, even including suicidality, anxiety and panic attacks, crying, irritability and anger, lack of int
out of control are common. Assorted somatic symptoms include breast tenderness, bloating, headache and pain. Feelings of
and relationships, fatigue and tiredness, difficulty focusing or thinking, food cravings and binge eating, and feeling out of
including suicidality, anxiety and panic attacks, crying, irritability and anger, lack of interest in or attention to activities and r
somatic symptoms include breast tenderness, bloating, headache and pain. Feelings of sadness and despair, even including su
difficulty focusing or thinking, food cravings and binge eating, and feeling out of control are common. Assorted somatic s
attacks, crying, irritability and anger, lack of interest in or attention to activities and relationships, fatigue and tiredness, di
tenderness, bloating, headache and pain. Feelings of sadness and despair, even including suicidality, anxiety and panic attac
food cravings and binge eating, and feeling out of control are common. Assorted somatic symptoms include breast tenderne
lack of interest in or attention to activities and relationships, fatigue and tiredness, difficulty focusing or thinking, food cravi
Feelings of sadness and despair, even including suicidality, anxiety and panic attacks, crying, irritability and anger, lack of int
out of control are common. Assorted somatic symptoms include breast tenderness, bloating, headache and pain. Feelings of
and relationships, fatigue and tiredness, difficulty focusing or thinking, food cravings and binge eating, and feeling out of
including suicidality, anxiety and panic attacks, crying, irritability and anger, lack of interest in or attention to activities and r
somatic symptoms include breast tenderness, bloating, headache and pain. Feelings of sadness and despair, even including su
difficulty focusing or thinking, food cravings and binge eating, and feeling out of control are common. Assorted somatic s
attacks, crying, irritability and anger, lack of interest in or attention to activities and relationships, fatigue and tiredness, di
tenderness, bloating, headache and pain. Feelings of sadness and despair, even including suicidality, anxiety and panic attac
food cravings and binge eating, and feeling out of control are common. Assorted somatic symptoms include breast tenderne
lack of interest in or attention to activities and relationships, fatigue and tiredness, difficulty focusing or thinking, food cravi
Feelings of sadness and despair, even including suicidality, anxiety and panic attacks, crying, irritability and anger, lack of int
out of control are common. Assorted somatic symptoms include breast tenderness, bloating, headache and pain. Feelings of
and relationships, fatigue and tiredness, difficulty focusing or thinking, food cravings and binge eating, and feeling out of
including suicidality, anxiety and panic attacks, crying, irritability and anger, lack of interest in or attention to activities and r
somatic symptoms include breast tenderness, bloating, headache and pain. Feelings of sadness and despair, even including su
difficulty focusing or thinking, food cravings and binge eating, and feeling out of control are common. Assorted somatic a
attacks, crying, irritability and anger, lack of interest in or attention to activities and relationships, fatigue and tiredness, di
tenderness, bloating, headache and pain. Feelings of sadness and despair, even including suicidality, anxiety and panic attac
food cravings and binge eating, and feeling out of control are common. Assorted somatic symptoms include breast tenderne
lack of interest in or attention to activities and relationships, fatigue and tiredness, difficulty focusing or thinking, food cravi
Feelings of sadness and despair, even including suicidality, anxiety and panic attacks, crying, irritability and anger, lack of int
out of control are common. Assorted somatic symptoms include breast tenderness, bloating, headache and pain. Feelings of
and relationships, fatigue and tiredness, difficulty focusing or thinking, food cravings and binge eating, and feeling out of
including suicidality, anxiety and panic attacks, crying, irritability and anger, lack of interest in or attention to activities and r
somatic symptoms include breast tenderness, bloating, headache and pain. Feelings of sadness and despair, even including su
difficulty focusing or thinking, food cravings and binge eating, and feeling out of control are common. Assorted somatic
attacks, crying, irritability and anger, lack of interest in or attention to activities and relationships, fatigue and tiredness, di
tenderness, bloating, headache and pain. Feelings of sadness and despair, even including suicidality, anxiety and panic attac
food cravings and binge eating, and feeling out of control are common. Assorted somatic symptoms include breast tenderne
lack of interest in or attention to activities and relationships, fatigue and tiredness, difficulty focusing or thinking, food crav
Feelings of sadness and despair, even including suicidality, anxiety and panic attacks, crying, irritability and anger, lack of int
out of control are common. Assorted somatic symptoms include breast tenderness, bloating, headache and pain. Feelings of
and relationships, fatigue and tiredness, difficulty focusing or thinking, food cravings and binge eating, and feeling out of
including suicidality, anxiety and panic attacks, crying, irritability and anger, lack of interest in or attention to activities a

activities and relationships, fatigue and tiredness, difficulty focusing or thinking, food cravings and binge eating, and feeling
even including suicidality, anxiety and panic attacks, crying, irritability and anger, lack of interest in or attention to activities
Assorted somatic symptoms include breast tenderness, bloating, headache and pain. Feelings of sadness and despair, even
nd tiredness, difficulty focusing or thinking, food cravings and binge eating, and feeling out of control are common. Assorted
panic attacks, crying, irritability and anger, lack of interest in or attention to activities and relationships, fatigue and tiredness,
east tenderness, bloating, headache and pain. Feelings of sadness and despair, even including suicidality, anxiety and panic
inking, food cravings and binge eating, and feeling out of control are common. Assorted somatic symptoms include breast
and anger, lack of interest in or attention to activities and relationships, fatigue and tiredness, difficulty focusing or thinking,
and pain. Feelings of sadness and despair, even including suicidality, anxiety and panic attacks, crying, irritability and anger,
and feeling out of control are common. Assorted somatic symptoms include breast tenderness, bloating, headache and pain.
activities and relationships, fatigue and tiredness, difficulty focusing or thinking, food cravings and binge eating, and feeling
even including suicidality, anxiety and panic attacks, crying, irritability and anger, lack of interest in or attention to activities
Assorted somatic symptoms include breast tenderness, bloating, headache and pain. Feelings of sadness and despair, even
nd tiredness, difficulty focusing or thinking, food cravings and binge eating, and feeling out of control are common. Assorted
panic attacks, crying, irritability and anger, lack of interest in or attention to activities and relationships, fatigue and tiredness,
east tenderness, bloating, headache and pain. Feelings of sadness and despair, even including suicidality, anxiety and panic
inking, food cravings and binge eating, and feeling out of control are common. Assorted somatic symptoms include breast
and anger, lack of interest in or attention to activities and relationships, fatigue and tiredness, difficulty focusing or thinking,
and pain. Feelings of sadness and despair, even including suicidality, anxiety and panic attacks, crying, irritability and anger,
and feeling out of control are common. Assorted somatic symptoms include breast tenderness, bloating, headache and pain.
activities and relationships, fatigue and tiredness, difficulty focusing or thinking, food cravings and binge eating, and feeling
even including suicidality, anxiety and panic attacks, crying, irritability and anger, lack of interest in or attention to activities
Assorted somatic symptoms include breast tenderness, bloating, headache and pain. Feelings of sadness and despair, even
nd tiredness, difficulty focusing or thinking, food cravings and binge eating, and feeling out of control are common. Assorted
panic attacks, crying, irritability and anger, lack of interest in or attention to activities and relationships, fatigue and tiredness,
east tenderness, bloating, headache and pain. Feelings of sadness and despair, even including suicidality, anxiety and panic
inking, food cravings and binge eating, and feeling out of control are common. Assorted somatic symptoms include breast
and anger, lack of interest in or attention to activities and relationships, fatigue and tiredness, difficulty focusing or thinking,
and pain. Feelings of sadness and despair, even including suicidality, anxiety and panic attacks, crying, irritability and anger,
and feeling out of control are common. Assorted somatic symptoms include breast tenderness, bloating, headache and pain.
activities and relationships, fatigue and tiredness, difficulty focusing or thinking, food cravings and binge eating, and feeling
even including suicidality, anxiety and panic attacks, crying, irritability and anger, lack of interest in or attention to activities
Assorted somatic symptoms include breast tenderness, bloating, headache and pain. Feelings of sadness and despair, even
nd tiredness, difficulty focusing or thinking, food cravings and binge eating, and feeling out of control are common. Assorted
panic attacks, crying, irritability and anger, lack of interest in or attention to activities and relationships, fatigue and tiredness,
east tenderness, bloating, headache and pain. Feelings of sadness and despair, even including suicidality, anxiety and panic
inking, food cravings and binge eating, and feeling out of control are common. Assorted somatic symptoms include breast
and anger, lack of interest in or attention to activities and relationships, fatigue and tiredness, difficulty focusing or thinking,
and pain. Feelings of sadness and despair, even including suicidality, anxiety and panic attacks, crying, irritability and anger,
and feeling out of control are common. Assorted somatic symptoms include breast tenderness, bloating, headache and pain.
activities and relationships, fatigue and tiredness, difficulty focusing or thinking, food cravings and binge eating, and feeling
even including suicidality, anxiety and panic attacks, crying, irritability and anger, lack of interest in or attention to activities
Assorted somatic symptoms include breast tenderness, bloating, headache and pain. Feelings of sadness and despair, even
nd tiredness, difficulty focusing or thinking, food cravings and binge eating, and feeling out of control are common. Assorted
panic attacks, crying, irritability and anger, lack of interest in or attention to activities and relationships, fatigue and tiredness,
east tenderness, bloating, headache and pain. Feelings of sadness and despair, even including suicidality, anxiety and panic
inking, food cravings and binge eating, and feeling out of control are common. Assorted somatic symptoms include breast
and anger, lack of interest in or attention to activities and relationships, fatigue and tiredness, difficulty focusing or thinking,
and pain. Feelings of sadness and despair, even including suicidality, anxiety and panic attacks, crying, irritability and anger,
and feeling out of control are common. Assorted somatic symptoms include breast tenderness, bloating, headache and pain.
activities and relationships, fatigue and tiredness, difficulty focusing or thinking, food cravings and binge eating, and feeling
even including suicidality, anxiety and panic attacks, crying, irritability and anger, lack of interest in or attention to activities
Assorted somatic symptoms include breast tenderness, bloating, headache and pain. Feelings of sadness and despair, even
gue and tiredness, difficulty focusing or thinking, food cravings and binge eating, and feeling out of control are common.

Feelings of sadness and despair, even including suicidality, anxiety and panic attacks, crying, irritability and anger, lack of inte
out of control are common. Assorted somatic symptoms include breast tenderness, bloating, headache and pain. Feelings of
and relationships, fatigue and tiredness, difficulty focusing or thinking, food cravings and binge eating, and feeling out of
including suicidality, anxiety and panic attacks, crying, irritability and anger, lack of interest in or attention to activities and re
somatic symptoms include breast tenderness, bloating, headache and pain. Feelings of sadness and despair, even including su
difficulty focusing or thinking, food cravings and binge eating, and feeling out of control are common. Assorted somatic s
attacks, crying, irritability and anger, lack of interest in or attention to activities and relationships, fatigue and tiredness, di
tenderness, bloating, headache and pain. Feelings of sadness and despair, even including suicidality, anxiety and panic attack
food cravings and binge eating, and feeling out of control are common. Assorted somatic symptoms include breast tendernes
lack of interest in or attention to activities and relationships, fatigue and tiredness, difficulty focusing or thinking, food cravi
Feelings of sadness and despair, even including suicidality, anxiety and panic attacks, crying, irritability and anger, lack of inte
out of control are common. Assorted somatic symptoms include breast tenderness, bloating, headache and pain. Feelings of
and relationships, fatigue and tiredness, difficulty focusing or thinking, food cravings and binge eating, and feeling out of
including suicidality, anxiety and panic attacks, crying, irritability and anger, lack of interest in or attention to activities and re
somatic symptoms include breast tenderness, bloating, headache and pain. Feelings of sadness and despair, even including su
difficulty focusing or thinking, food cravings and binge eating, and feeling out of control are common. Assorted somatic s
attacks, crying, irritability and anger, lack of interest in or attention to activities and relationships, fatigue and tiredness, di
tenderness, bloati 3500 days d pain. Feelings of sadness and despair, even including suicidality, anxiety and panic attack
food cravings and binge eating, and feeling out of control are common. Assorted somatic symptoms include breast tendernes
lack of interest in or attention to activities and relationships, fatigue and tiredness, difficulty focusing or thinking, food cravi
Feelings of sadness and despair, even including suicidality, anxiety and panic attacks, crying, irritability and anger, lack of inte
out of control are common. Assorted somatic symptoms include breast tenderness, bloating, headache and pain. Feelings of
and relationships, fatigue and tiredness, difficulty focusing or thinking, food cravings and binge eating, and feeling out of
including suicidality, anxiety and panic attacks, crying, irritability and anger, lack of interest in or attention to activities and re
somatic symptoms include breast tenderness, bloating, headache and pain. Feelings of sadness and despair, even including su
difficulty focusing or thinking, food cravings and binge eating, and feeling out of control are common. Assorted somatic s
attacks, crying, irritability and anger, lack of interest in or attention to activities and relationships, fatigue and tiredness, di
tenderness, bloating, headache and pain. Feelings of sadness and despair, even including suicidality, anxiety and panic attack
food cravings and binge eating, and feeling out of control are common. Assorted somatic symptoms include breast tendernes
lack of interest in or attention to activities and relationships, fatigue and tiredness, difficulty focusing or thinking, food cravi
Feelings of sadness and despair, even including suicidality, anxiety and panic attacks, crying, irritability and anger, lack of inte
out of control are common. Assorted somatic symptoms include breast tenderness, bloating, headache and pain. Feelings of
and relationships, fatigue and tiredness, difficulty focusing or thinking, food cravings and binge eating, and feeling out of
including suicidality, anxiety and panic attacks, crying, irritability and anger, lack of interest in or attention to activities and re
somatic symptoms include breast tenderness, bloating, headache and pain. Feelings of sadness and despair, even including su
difficulty focusing or thinking, food cravings and binge eating, and feeling out of control are common. Assorted somatic s
attacks, crying, irritability and anger, lack of interest in or attention to activities and relationships, fatigue and tiredness, di
tenderness, bloating, headache and pain. Feelings of sadness and despair, even including suicidality, anxiety and panic attack
food cravings and binge eating, and feeling out of control are common. Assorted somatic symptoms include breast tendernes
lack of interest in or attention to activities and relationships, fatigue and tiredness, difficulty focusing or thinking, food cravi
Feelings of sadness and despair, even including suicidality, anxiety and panic attacks, crying, irritability and anger, lack of inte
out of control are common. Assorted somatic symptoms include breast tenderness, bloating, headache and pain. Feelings of
and relationships, fatigue and tiredness, difficulty focusing or thinking, food cravings and binge eating, and feeling out of
including suicidality, anxiety and panic attacks, crying, irritability and anger, lack of interest in or attention to activities and re
somatic symptoms include breast tenderness, bloating, headache and pain. Feelings of sadness and despair, even including su
difficulty focusing or thinking, food cravings and binge eating, and feeling out of control are common. Assorted somatic s
attacks, crying, irritability and anger, lack of interest in or attention to activities and relationships, fatigue and tiredness, di
tenderness, bloating, headache and pain. Feelings of sadness and despair, even including suicidality, anxiety and panic attack
food cravings and binge eating, and feeling out of control are common. Assorted somatic symptoms include breast tendernes
lack of interest in or attention to activities and relationships, fatigue and tiredness, difficulty focusing or thinking, food cravi
Feelings of sadness and despair, even including suicidality, anxiety and panic attacks, crying, irritability and anger, lack of int
out of control are common. Assorted somatic symptoms include breast tenderness, bloating, headache and pain. Feelings of
and relationships, fatigue and tiredness, difficulty focusing or thinking, food cravings and binge eating, and feeling out of
including suicidality, anxiety and panic attacks, crying, irritability and anger, lack of interest in or attention to activities and re
somatic symptoms include breast tenderness, bloating, headache and pain. Feelings of sadness and despair, even including su
difficulty focusing or thinking, food cravings and binge eating, and feeling out of control are common. Assorted somatic s
attacks, crying, irritability and anger, lack of interest in or attention to activities and relationships, fatigue and tiredness, di
tenderness, bloating, headache and pain. Feelings of sadness and despair, even including suicidality, anxiety and panic attack
food cravings and binge eating, and feeling out of control are common. Assorted somatic symptoms include breast tendernes
lack of interest in or attention to activities and relationships, fatigue and tiredness, difficulty focusing or thinking, food cravi
Feelings of sadness and despair, even including suicidality, anxiety and panic attacks, crying, irritability and anger, lack of int
out of control are common. Assorted somatic symptoms include breast tenderness, bloating, headache and pain. Feelings of
and relationships, fatigue and tiredness, difficulty focusing or thinking, food cravings and binge eating, and feeling out of
including suicidality, anxiety and panic attacks, crying, irritability and anger, lack of interest in or attention to activities a

activities and relationships, fatigue and tiredness, difficulty focusing or thinking, food cravings and binge eating, and feeling even including suicidality, anxiety and panic attacks, crying, irritability and anger, lack of interest in or attention to activities Assorted somatic symptoms include breast tenderness, bloating, headache and pain. Feelings of sadness and despair, even nd tiredness, difficulty focusing or thinking, food cravings and binge eating, and feeling out of control are common. Assorted panic attacks, crying, irritability and anger, lack of interest in or attention to activities and relationships, fatigue and tiredness, ast tenderness, bloating, headache and pain. Feelings of sadness and despair, even including suicidality, anxiety and panic inking, food cravings and binge eating, and feeling out of control are common. Assorted somatic symptoms include breast nd anger, lack of interest in or attention to activities and relationships, fatigue and tiredness, difficulty focusing or thinking, and pain. Feelings of sadness and despair, even including suicidality, anxiety and panic attacks, crying, irritability and anger, and feeling out of control are common. Assorted somatic symptoms include breast tenderness, bloating, headache and pain.
activities and relationships, fatigue and tiredness, difficulty focusing or thinking, food cravings and binge eating, and feeling even including suicidality, anxiety and panic attacks, crying, irritability and anger, lack of interest in or attention to activities Assorted somatic symptoms include breast tenderness, bloating, headache and pain. Feelings of sadness and despair, even nd tiredness, difficulty focusing or thinking, food cravings and binge eating, and feeling out of control are common. Assorted panic attacks, crying, irritability and anger, lack of interest in or attention to activities and relationships, fatigue and tiredness, ast tenderness, bloating, headache and pain. Feelings of sadness and despair, even including suicidality, anxiety and panic inking, food cravings and binge eating, and feeling out of control are common. Assorted somatic symptoms include breast nd anger, lack of interest in or attention to activities and relationships, fatigue and tiredness, difficulty focusing or thinking, and pain. Feelings of sadness and despair, even including suicidality, anxiety and panic attacks, crying, irritability and anger, and feeling out of control are common. Assorted somatic symptoms include breast tenderness, bloating, headache and pain.
activities and relationships, fatigue and tiredness, difficulty focusing or thinking, food cravings and binge eating, and feeling ven including suicidality, anxiety and panic attacks, crying, irritability and anger, lack of interest in or attention to activities Assorted somatic symptoms include breast tenderness, bloating, headache and pain. Feelings of sadness and despair, even d tiredness, difficulty focusing or thinking, food cravings and binge eating, and feeling out of control are common. Assorted panic attacks, crying, irritability and anger, lack of interest in or attention to activities and relationships, fatigue and tiredness, ast tenderness, bloating, headache and pain. Feelings of sadness and despair, even including suicidality, anxiety and panic inking, food cravings and binge eating, and feeling out of control are common. Assorted somatic symptoms include breast nd anger, lack of interest in or attention to activities and relationships, fatigue and tiredness, difficulty focusing or thinking, and pain. Feelings of sadness and despair, even including suicidality, anxiety and panic attacks, crying, irritability and anger, and feeling out of control are common. Assorted somatic symptoms include breast tenderness, bloating, headache and pain.
activities and relationships, fatigue and tiredness, difficulty focusing or thinking, food cravings and binge eating, and feeling ven including suicidality, anxiety and panic attacks, crying, irritability and anger, lack of interest in or attention to activities Assorted somatic symptoms include breast tenderness, bloating, headache and pain. Feelings of sadness and despair, even d tiredness, difficulty focusing or thinking, food cravings and binge eating, and feeling out of control are common. Assorted panic attacks, crying, irritability and anger, lack of interest in or attention to activities and relationships, fatigue and tiredness, ast tenderness, bloating, headache and pain. Feelings of sadness and despair, even including suicidality, anxiety and panic nking, food cravings and binge eating, and feeling out of control are common. Assorted somatic symptoms include breast nd anger, lack of interest in or attention to activities and relationships, fatigue and tiredness, difficulty focusing or thinking, and pain. Feelings of sadness and despair, even including suicidality, anxiety and panic attacks, crying, irritability and anger, and feeling out of control are common. Assorted somatic symptoms include breast tenderness, bloating, headache and pain.
activities and relationships, fatigue and tiredness, difficulty focusing or thinking, food cravings and binge eating, and feeling ven including suicidality, anxiety and panic attacks, crying, irritability and anger, lack of interest in or attention to activities Assorted somatic symptoms include breast tenderness, bloating, headache and pain. Feelings of sadness and despair, even d tiredness, difficulty focusing or thinking, food cravings and binge eating, and feeling out of control are common. Assorted anic attacks, crying, irritability and anger, lack of interest in or attention to activities and relationships, fatigue and tiredness, ast tenderness, bloating, headache and pain. Feelings of sadness and despair, even including suicidality, anxiety and panic nking, food cravings and binge eating, and feeling out of control are common. Assorted somatic symptoms include breast nd anger, lack of interest in or attention to activities and relationships, fatigue and tiredness, difficulty focusing or thinking, and pain. Feelings of sadness and despair, even including suicidality, anxiety and panic attacks, crying, irritability and anger, nd feeling out of control are common. Assorted somatic symptoms include breast tenderness, bloating, headache and pain.
activities and relationships, fatigue and tiredness, difficulty focusing or thinking, food cravings and binge eating, and feeling ven including suicidality, anxiety and panic attacks, crying, irritability and anger, lack of interest in or attention to activities Assorted somatic symptoms include breast tenderness, bloating, headache and pain. Feelings of sadness and despair, even d tiredness, difficulty focusing or thinking, food cravings and binge eating, and feeling out of control are common. Assorted anic attacks, crying, irritability and anger, lack of interest in or attention to activities and relationships, fatigue and tiredness, ast tenderness, bloating, headache and pain. Feelings of sadness and despair, even including suicidality, anxiety and panic nking, food cravings and binge eating, and feeling out of control are common. Assorted somatic symptoms include breast nd anger, lack of interest in or attention to activities and relationships, fatigue and tiredness, difficulty focusing or thinking, and pain. Feelings of sadness and despair, even including suicidality, anxiety and panic attacks, crying, irritability and anger, nd feeling out of control are common. Assorted somatic symptoms include breast tenderness, bloating, headache and pain.
activities and relationships, fatigue and tiredness, difficulty focusing or thinking, food cravings and binge eating, and feeling ven including suicidality, anxiety and panic attacks, crying, irritability and anger, lack of interest in or attention to activities Assorted somatic symptoms include breast tenderness, bloating, headache and pain. Feelings of sadness and despair, even ie and tiredness, difficulty focusing or thinking, food cravings and binge eating, and feeling out of control are common.

Feelings of sadness and despair, even including suicidality, anxiety and panic attacks, crying, irritability and anger, lack of int
out of control are common. Assorted somatic symptoms include breast tenderness, bloating, headache and pain. Feelings o
and relationships, fatigue and tiredness, difficulty focusing or thinking, food cravings and binge eating, and feeling out of
including suicidality, anxiety and panic attacks, crying, irritability and anger, lack of interest in or attention to activities and
somatic symptoms include breast tenderness, bloating, headache and pain. Feelings of sadness and despair, even including su
difficulty focusing or thinking, food cravings and binge eating, and feeling out of control are common. Assorted somatic
attacks, crying, irritability and anger, lack of interest in or attention to activities and relationships, fatigue and tiredness, d
tenderness, bloating, headache and pain. Feelings of sadness and despair, even including suicidality, anxiety and panic attac
food cravings and binge eating, and feeling out of control are common. Assorted somatic symptoms include breast tenderne
lack of interest in or attention to activities and relationships, fatigue and tiredness, difficulty focusing or thinking, food crav
Feelings of sadness and despair, even including suicidality, anxiety and panic attacks, crying, irritability and anger, lack of in
out of control are common. Assorted somatic symptoms include breast tenderness, bloating, headache and pain. Feelings o
and relationships, fatigue and tiredness, difficulty focusing or thinking, food cravings and binge eating, and feeling out of
including suicidality, anxiety and panic attacks, crying, irritability and anger, lack of interest in or attention to activities and
somatic symptoms include breast tenderness, bloating, headache and pain. Feelings of sadness and despair, even including su
difficulty focusing or thinking, food cravings and binge eating, and feeling out of control are common. Assorted somatic
attacks, crying, irritability and anger, lack of interest in or attention to activities and relationships, fatigue and tiredness, d
tenderness, bloating, headache and pain. Feelings of sadness and despair, even including suicidality, anxiety and panic attac
food cravings and binge eating, and feeling out of control are common. Assorted somatic symptoms include breast tenderne
lack of interest in or attention to activities and relationships, fatigue and tiredness, difficulty focusing or thinking, food crav
Feelings of sadness and despair, even including suicidality, anxiety and panic attacks, crying, irritability and anger, lack of in
out of control are common. Assorted somatic symptoms include breast tenderness, bloating, headache and pain. Feelings o
and relationships, fatigue and tiredness, difficulty focusing or thinking, food cravings and binge eating, and feeling out of
including suicidality, anxiety and panic attacks, crying, irritability and anger, lack of interest in or attention to activities and
somatic symptoms include breast tenderness, bloating, headache and pain. Feelings of sadness and despair, even including s
difficulty focusing or thinking, food cravings and binge eating, and feeling out of control are common. Assorted somatic
attacks, crying, irritability and anger, lack of interest in or attention to activities and relationships, fatigue and tiredness, d
tenderness, bloating, headache and pain. Feelings of sadness and despair, even including suicidality, anxiety and panic attac
food cravings and binge eating, and feeling out of control are common. Assorted somatic symptoms include breast tenderne
lack of interest in or attention to activities and relationships, fatigue and tiredness, difficulty focusing or thinking, food crav
Feelings of sadness and despair, even including suicidality, anxiety and panic attacks, crying, irritability and anger, lack of in
out of control are common. Assorted somatic symptoms include breast tenderness, bloating, headache and pain. Feelings o
and relationships, fatigue and tiredness, difficulty focusing or thinking, food cravings and binge eating, and feeling out of
including suicidality, anxiety and panic attacks, crying, irritability and anger, lack of interest in or attention to activities and
somatic symptoms include breast tenderness, bloating, headache and pain. Feelings of sadness and despair, even including s
difficulty focusing or thinking, food cravings and binge eating, and feeling out of control are common. Assorted somatic
attacks, crying, irritability and anger, lack of interest in or attention to activities and relationships, fatigue and tiredness, d
tenderness, bloating, headache and pain. Feelings of sadness and despair, even including suicidality, anxiety and panic atta
food cravings and binge eating, and feeling out of control are common. Assorted somatic symptoms include breast tenderne
lack of interest in or attention to activities and relationships, fatigue and tiredness, difficulty focusing or thinking, food crav
Feelings of sadness and despair, even including suicidality, anxiety and panic attacks, crying, irritability and anger, lack of in
out of control are common. Assorted somatic symptoms include breast tenderness, bloating, headache and pain. Feelings c
and relationships, fatigue and tiredness, difficulty focusing or thinking, food cravings and binge eating, and feeling out of
including suicidality, anxiety and panic attacks, crying, irritability and anger, lack of interest in or attention to activities and
somatic symptoms include breast tenderness, bloating, headache and pain. Feelings of sadness and despair, even including s
difficulty focusing or thinking, food cravings and binge eating, and feeling out of control are common. Assorted somatic
attacks, crying, irritability and anger, lack of interest in or attention to activities and relationships, fatigue and tiredness, c
tenderness, bloating, headache and pain. Feelings of sadness and despair, even including suicidality, anxiety and panic atta
food cravings and binge eating, and feeling out of control are common. Assorted somatic symptoms include breast tendern
lack of interest in or attention to activities and relationships, fatigue and tiredness, difficulty focusing or thinking, food crav
Feelings of sadness and despair, even including suicidality, anxiety and panic attacks, crying, irritability and anger, lack of in
out of control are common. Assorted somatic symptoms include breast tenderness, bloating, headache and pain. Feelings c
and relationships, fatigue and tiredness, difficulty focusing or thinking, food cravings and binge eating, and feeling out o
including suicidality, anxiety and panic attacks, crying, irritability and anger, lack of interest in or attention to activities and
somatic symptoms include breast tenderness, bloating, headache and pain. Feelings of sadness and despair, even including s
difficulty focusing or thinking, food cravings and binge eating, and feeling out of control are common. Assorted somatic
attacks, crying, irritability and anger, lack of interest in or attention to activities and relationships, fatigue and tiredness, c
tenderness, bloating, headache and pain. Feelings of sadness and despair, even including suicidality, anxiety and panic atta
food cravings and binge eating, and feeling out of control are common. Assorted somatic symptoms include breast tendern
lack of interest in or attention to activities and relationships, fatigue and tiredness, difficulty focusing or thinking, food crav
Feelings of sadness and despair, even including suicidality, anxiety and panic attacks, crying, irritability and anger, lack of in
out of control are common. Assorted somatic symptoms include breast tenderness, bloating, headache and pain. Feelings c
and relationships, fatigue and tiredness, difficulty focusing or thinking, food cravings and binge eating, and feeling out o
including suicidality, anxiety and panic attacks, crying, irritability and anger, lack of interest in or attention to activities

activities and relationships, fatigue and tiredness, difficulty focusing or thinking, food cravings and binge eating, and feeling even including suicidality, anxiety and panic attacks, crying, irritability and anger, lack of interest in or attention to activities Assorted somatic symptoms include breast tenderness, bloating, headache and pain. Feelings of sadness and despair, even and tiredness, difficulty focusing or thinking, food cravings and binge eating, and feeling out of control are common. Assorted panic attacks, crying, irritability and anger, lack of interest in or attention to activities and relationships, fatigue and tiredness, ast tenderness, bloating, headache and pain. Feelings of sadness and despair, even including suicidality, anxiety and panic inking, food cravings and binge eating, and feeling out of control are common. Assorted somatic symptoms include breast and anger, lack of interest in or attention to activities and relationships, fatigue and tiredness, difficulty focusing or thinking, and pain. Feelings of sadness and despair, even including suicidality, anxiety and panic attacks, crying, irritability and anger, and feeling out of control are common. Assorted somatic symptoms include breast tenderness, bloating, headache and pain. activities and relationships, fatigue and tiredness, difficulty focusing or thinking, food cravings and binge eating, and feeling even including suicidality, anxiety and panic attacks, crying, irritability and anger, lack of interest in or attention to activities Assorted somatic symptoms include breast tenderness, bloating, headache and pain. Feelings of sadness and despair, even and tiredness, difficulty focusing or thinking, food cravings and binge eating, and feeling out of control are common. Assorted panic attacks, crying, irritability and anger, lack of interest in or attention to activities and relationships, fatigue and tiredness, ast tenderness, bloating, headache and pain. Feelings of sadness and despair, even including suicidality, anxiety and panic inking, food cravings and binge eating, and feeling out of control are common. Assorted somatic symptoms include breast and anger, lack of interest in or attention to activities and relationships, fatigue and tiredness, difficulty focusing or thinking, and pain. Feelings of sadness and despair, even including suicidality, anxiety and panic attacks, crying, irritability and anger, and feeling out of control are common. Assorted somatic symptoms include breast tenderness, bloating, headache and pain. activities and relationships, fatigue and tiredness, difficulty focusing or thinking, food cravings and binge eating, and feeling even including suicidality, anxiety and panic attacks, crying, irritability and anger, lack of interest in or attention to activities Assorted somatic symptoms include breast tenderness, bloating, headache and pain. Feelings of sadness and despair, even and tiredness, difficulty focusing or thinking, food cravings and binge eating, and feeling out of control are common. Assorted panic attacks, crying, irritability and anger, lack of interest in or attention to activities and relationships, fatigue and tiredness, ast tenderness, bloating, headache and pain. Feelings of sadness and despair, even including suicidality, anxiety and panic inking, food cravings and binge eating, and feeling out of control are common. Assorted somatic symptoms include breast and anger, lack of interest in or attention to activities and relationships, fatigue and tiredness, difficulty focusing or thinking, and pain. Feelings of sadness and despair, even including suicidality, anxiety and panic attacks, crying, irritability and anger, and feeling out of control are common. Assorted somatic symptoms include breast tenderness, bloating, headache and pain. activities and relationships, fatigue and tiredness, difficulty focusing or thinking, food cravings and binge eating, and feeling even including suicidality, anxiety and panic attacks, crying, irritability and anger, lack of interest in or attention to activities Assorted somatic symptoms include breast tenderness, bloating, headache and pain. Feelings of sadness and despair, even and tiredness, difficulty focusing or thinking, food cravings and binge eating, and feeling out of control are common. Assorted panic attacks, crying, irritability and anger, lack of interest in or attention to activities and relationships, fatigue and tiredness, ast tenderness, bloating, headache and pain. Feelings of sadness and despair, even including suicidality, anxiety and panic inking, food cravings and binge eating, and feeling out of control are common. Assorted somatic symptoms include breast and anger, lack of interest in or attention to activities and relationships, fatigue and tiredness, difficulty focusing or thinking, and pain. Feelings of sadness and despair, even including suicidality, anxiety and panic attacks, crying, irritability and anger, and feeling out of control are common. Assorted somatic symptoms include breast tenderness, bloating, headache and pain. activities and relationships, fatigue and tiredness, difficulty focusing or thinking, food cravings and binge eating, and feeling even including suicidality, anxiety and panic attacks, crying, irritability and anger, lack of interest in or attention to activities Assorted somatic symptoms include breast tenderness, bloating, headache and pain. Feelings of sadness and despair, even and tiredness, difficulty focusing or thinking, food cravings and binge eating, and feeling out of control are common. Assorted panic attacks, crying, irritability and anger, lack of interest in or attention to activities and relationships, fatigue and tiredness, ast tenderness, bloating, headache and pain. Feelings of sadness and despair, even including suicidality, anxiety and panic inking, food cravings and binge eating, and feeling out of control are common. Assorted somatic symptoms include breast nd anger, lack of interest in or attention to activities and relationships, fatigue and tiredness, difficulty focusing or thinking, and pain. Feelings of sadness and despair, even including suicidality, anxiety and panic attacks, crying, irritability and anger, and feeling out of control are common. Assorted somatic symptoms include breast tenderness, bloating, headache and pain. activities and relationships, fatigue and tiredness, difficulty focusing or thinking, food cravings and binge eating, and feeling ven including suicidality, anxiety and panic attacks, crying, irritability and anger, lack of interest in or attention to activities Assorted somatic symptoms include breast tenderness, bloating, headache and pain. Feelings of sadness and despair, even ue and tiredness, difficulty focusing or thinking, food cravings and binge eating, and feeling out of control are common.

Feelings of sadness and despair, even including suicidality, anxiety and panic attacks, crying, irritability and anger, lack of int
out of control are common. Assorted somatic symptoms include breast tenderness, bloating, headache and pain. Feelings of
and relationships, fatigue and tiredness, difficulty focusing or thinking, food cravings and binge eating, and feeling out of
including suicidality, anxiety and panic attacks, crying, irritability and anger, lack of interest in or attention to activities and r
somatic symptoms include breast tenderness, bloating, headache and pain. Feelings of sadness and despair, even including su
difficulty focusing or thinking, food cravings and binge eating, and feeling out of control are common. Assorted somatic s
attacks, crying, irritability and anger, lack of interest in or attention to activities and relationships, fatigue and tiredness, di
tenderness, bloating, headache and pain. Feelings of sadness and despair, even including suicidality, anxiety and panic attack
food cravings and binge eating, and feeling out of control are common. Assorted somatic symptoms include breast tenderne
lack of interest in or attention to activities and relationships, fatigue and tiredness, difficulty focusing or thinking, food cravi
Feelings of sadness and despair, even including suicidality, anxiety and panic attacks, crying, irritability and anger, lack of int
out of control are common. Assorted somatic symptoms include breast tenderness, bloating, headache and pain. Feelings of
and relationships, fatigue and tiredness, difficulty focusing or thinking, food cravings and binge eating, and feeling out of
including suicidality, anxiety and panic attacks, crying, irritability and anger, lack of interest in or attention to activities and r
somatic symptoms include breast tenderness, bloating, headache and pain. Feelings of sadness and despair, even including su
difficulty focusing or thinking, food cravings and binge eating, and feeling out of control are common. Assorted somatic s
attacks, crying, irritability and anger, lack of interest in or attention to activities and relationships, fatigue and tiredness, di
tenderness, bloating, headache and pain. Feelings of sadness and despair, even including suicidality, anxiety and panic attac
food cravings and binge eating, and feeling out of control are common. Assorted somatic symptoms include breast tenderne
lack of interest in or attention to activities and relationships, fatigue and tiredness, difficulty focusing or thinking, food cravi
Feelings of sadness and despair, even including suicidality, anxiety and panic attacks, crying, irritability and anger, lack of int
out of control are common. Assorted somatic symptoms include breast tenderness, bloating, headache and pain. Feelings of
and relationships, fatigue and tiredness, difficulty focusing or thinking, food cravings and binge eating, and feeling out of
including suicidality, anxiety and panic attacks, crying, irritability and anger, lack of interest in or attention to activities and r
somatic symptoms include breast tenderness, bloating, headache and pain. Feelings of sadness and despair, even including su
difficulty focusing or thinking, food cravings and binge eating, and feeling out of control are common. Assorted somatic
attacks, crying, irritability and anger, lack of interest in or attention to activities and relationships, fatigue and tiredness, di
tenderness, bloating, headache and pain. Feelings of sadness and despair, even including suicidality, anxiety and panic attac
food cravings and binge eating, and feeling out of control are common. Assorted somatic symptoms include breast tenderne
lack of interest in or attention to activities and relationships, fatigue and tiredness, difficulty focusing or thinking, food crav
Feelings of sadness and despair, even including suicidality, anxiety and panic attacks, crying, irritability and anger, lack of int
out of control are common. Assorted somatic symptoms include breast tenderness, bloating, headache and pain. Feelings of
and relationships, fatigue and tiredness, difficulty focusing or thinking, food cravings and binge eating, and feeling out of
including suicidality, anxiety and panic attacks, crying, irritability and anger, lack of interest in or attention to activities and r
somatic symptoms include breast tenderness, bloating, headache and pain. Feelings of sadness and despair, even including su
difficulty focusing or thinking, food cravings and binge eating, and feeling out of control are common. Assorted somatic
attacks, crying, irritability and anger, lack of interest in or attention to activities and relationships, fatigue and tiredness, di
tenderness, bloating, headache and pain. Feelings of sadness and despair, even including suicidality, anxiety and panic attac
food cravings and binge eating, and feeling out of control are common. Assorted somatic symptoms include breast tenderne
lack of interest in or attention to activities and relationships, fatigue and tiredness, difficulty focusing or thinking, food crav
Feelings of sadness and despair, even including suicidality, anxiety and panic attacks, crying, irritability and anger, lack of int
out of control are common. Assorted somatic symptoms include breast tenderness, bloating, headache and pain. Feelings o
and relationships, fatigue and tiredness, difficulty focusing or thinking, food cravings and binge eating, and feeling out of
including suicidality, anxiety and panic attacks, crying, irritability and anger, lack of interest in or attention to activities and r
somatic symptoms include breast tenderness, bloating, headache and pain. Feelings of sadness and despair, even including su
difficulty focusing or thinking, food cravings and binge eating, and feeling out of control are common. Assorted somatic
attacks, crying, irritability and anger, lack of interest in or attention to activities and relationships, fatigue and tiredness, d
tenderness, bloating, headache and pain. Feelings of sadness and despair, even including suicidality, anxiety and panic attac
food cravings and binge eating, and feeling out of control are common. Assorted somatic symptoms include breast tenderne
lack of interest in or attention to activities and relationships, fatigue and tiredness, difficulty focusing or thinking, food crav
Feelings of sadness and despair, even including suicidality, anxiety and panic attacks, crying, irritability and anger, lack of in
out of control are common. Assorted somatic symptoms include breast tenderness, bloating, headache and pain. Feelings o
and relationships, fatigue and tiredness, difficulty focusing or thinking, food cravings and binge eating, and feeling out of
including suicidality, anxiety and panic attacks, crying, irritability and anger, lack of interest in or attention to activities and
somatic symptoms include breast tenderness, bloating, headache and pain. Feelings of sadness and despair, even including su
difficulty focusing or thinking, food cravings and binge eating, and feeling out of control are common. Assorted somatic
attacks, crying, irritability and anger, lack of interest in or attention to activities and relationships, fatigue and tiredness, d
tenderness, bloating, headache and pain. Feelings of sadness and despair, even including suicidality, anxiety and panic attac
food cravings and binge eating, and feeling out of control are common. Assorted somatic symptoms include breast tenderne
lack of interest in or attention to activities and relationships, fatigue and tiredness, difficulty focusing or thinking, food crav
Feelings of sadness and despair, even including suicidality, anxiety and panic attacks, crying, irritability and anger, lack of in
out of control are common. Assorted somatic symptoms include breast tenderness, bloating, headache and pain. Feelings o
and relationships, fatigue and tiredness, difficulty focusing or thinking, food cravings and binge eating, and feeling out of
including suicidality, anxiety and panic attacks, crying, irritability and anger, lack of interest in or attention to activities

activities and relationships, fatigue and tiredness, difficulty focusing or thinking, food cravings and binge eating, and feeling
even including suicidality, anxiety and panic attacks, crying, irritability and anger, lack of interest in or attention to activities
Assorted somatic symptoms include breast tenderness, bloating, headache and pain. Feelings of sadness and despair, even
nd tiredness, difficulty focusing or thinking, food cravings and binge eating, and feeling out of control are common. Assorted
panic attacks, crying, irritability and anger, lack of interest in or attention to activities and relationships, fatigue and tiredness,
east tenderness, bloating, headache and pain. Feelings of sadness and despair, even including suicidality, anxiety and panic
inking, food cravings and binge eating, and feeling out of control are common. Assorted somatic symptoms include breast
and anger, lack of interest in or attention to activities and relationships, fatigue and tiredness, difficulty focusing or thinking,
and pain. Feelings of sadness and despair, even including suicidality, anxiety and panic attacks, crying, irritability and anger,
and feeling out of control are common. Assorted somatic symptoms include breast tenderness, bloating, headache and pain.
activities and relationships, fatigue and tiredness, difficulty focusing or thinking, food cravings and binge eating, and feeling
even including suicidality, anxiety and panic attacks, crying, irritability and anger, lack of interest in or attention to activities
Assorted somatic symptoms include breast tenderness, bloating, headache and pain. Feelings of sadness and despair, even
nd tiredness, difficulty focusing or thinking, food cravings and binge eating, and feeling out of control are common. Assorted
panic attacks, crying, irritability and anger, lack of interest in or attention to activities and relationships, fatigue and tiredness,
east tenderness, bloating, headache and pain. Feelings of sadness and despair, even including suicidality, anxiety and panic
inking, food cravings and binge eating, and feeling out of control are common. Assorted somatic symptoms include breast
and anger, lack of interest in or attention to activities and relationships, fatigue and tiredness, difficulty focusing or thinking,
and pain. Feelings of sadness and despair, even including suicidality, anxiety and panic attacks, crying, irritability and anger,
and feeling out of control are common. Assorted somatic symptoms include breast tenderness, bloating, headache and pain.
activities and relationships, fatigue and tiredness, difficulty focusing or thinking, food cravings and binge eating, and feeling
even including suicidality, anxiety and panic attacks, crying, irritability and anger, lack of interest in or attention to activities
Assorted somatic symptoms include breast tenderness, bloating, headache and pain. Feelings of sadness and despair, even
nd tiredness, difficulty focusing or thinking, food cravings and binge eating, and feeling out of control are common. Assorted
panic attacks, crying, irritability and anger, lack of interest in or attention to activities and relationships, fatigue and tiredness,
east tenderness, bloating, headache and pain. Feelings of sadness and despair, even including suicidality, anxiety and panic
inking, food cravings and binge eating, and feeling out of control are common. Assorted somatic symptoms include breast
and anger, lack of interest in or attention to activities and relationships, fatigue and tiredness, difficulty focusing or thinking,
and pain. Feelings of sadness and despair, even including suicidality, anxiety and panic attacks, crying, irritability and anger,
and feeling out of control are common. Assorted somatic symptoms include breast tenderness, bloating, headache and pain.
activities and relationships, fatigue and tiredness, difficulty focusing or thinking, food cravings and binge eating, and feeling
even including suicidality, anxiety and panic attacks, crying, irritability and anger, lack of interest in or attention to activities
Assorted somatic symptoms include breast tenderness, bloating, headache and pain. Feelings of sadness and despair, even
nd tiredness, difficulty focusing or thinking, food cravings and binge eating, and feeling out of control are common. Assorted
panic attacks, crying, irritability and anger, lack of interest in or attention to activities and relationships, fatigue and tiredness,
east tenderness, bloating, headache and pain. Feelings of sadness and despair, even including suicidality, anxiety and panic
inking, food cravings and binge eating, and feeling out of control are common. Assorted somatic symptoms include breast
and anger, lack of interest in or attention to activities and relationships, fatigue and tiredness, difficulty focusing or thinking,
and pain. Feelings of sadness and despair, even including suicidality, anxiety and panic attacks, crying, irritability and anger,
and feeling out of control are common. Assorted somatic symptoms include breast tenderness, bloating, headache and pain.
activities and relationships, fatigue and tiredness, difficulty focusing or thinking, food cravings and binge eating, and feeling
even including suicidality, anxiety and panic attacks, crying, irritability and anger, lack of interest in or attention to activities
Assorted somatic symptoms include breast tenderness, bloating, headache and pain. Feelings of sadness and despair, even
nd tiredness, difficulty focusing or thinking, food cravings and binge eating, and feeling out of control are common. Assorted
panic attacks, crying, irritability and anger, lack of interest in or attention to activities and relationships, fatigue and tiredness,
east tenderness, bloating, headache and pain. Feelings of sadness and despair, even including suicidality, anxiety and panic
inking, food cravings and binge eating, and feeling out of control are common. Assorted somatic symptoms include breast
and anger, lack of interest in or attention to activities and relationships, fatigue and tiredness, difficulty focusing or thinking,
and pain. Feelings of sadness and despair, even including suicidality, anxiety and panic attacks, crying, irritability and anger,
and feeling out of control are common. Assorted somatic symptoms include breast tenderness, bloating, headache and pain.
activities and relationships, fatigue and tiredness, difficulty focusing or thinking, food cravings and binge eating, and feeling
even including suicidality, anxiety and panic attacks, crying, irritability and anger, lack of interest in or attention to activities
Assorted somatic symptoms include breast tenderness, bloating, headache and pain. Feelings of sadness and despair, even
igue and tiredness, difficulty focusing or thinking, food cravings and binge eating, and feeling out of control are common.

Feelings of sadness and despair, even including suicidality, anxiety and panic attacks, crying, irritability and anger, lack of int
out of control are common. Assorted somatic symptoms include breast tenderness, bloating, headache and pain. Feelings of
and relationships, fatigue and tiredness, difficulty focusing or thinking, food cravings and binge eating, and feeling out of
including suicidality, anxiety and panic attacks, crying, irritability and anger, lack of interest in or attention to activities and r
somatic symptoms include breast tenderness, bloating, headache and pain. Feelings of sadness and despair, even including su
difficulty focusing or thinking, food cravings and binge eating, and feeling out of control are common. Assorted somatic s
attacks, crying, irritability and anger, lack of interest in or attention to activities and relationships, fatigue and tiredness, di
tenderness, bloating, headache and pain. Feelings of sadness and despair, even including suicidality, anxiety and panic attac
food cravings and binge eating, and feeling out of control are common. Assorted somatic symptoms include breast tenderne
lack of interest in or attention to activities and relationships, fatigue and tiredness, difficulty focusing or thinking, food cravi
Feelings of sadness and despair, even including suicidality, anxiety and panic attacks, crying, irritability and anger, lack of int
out of control are common. Assorted somatic symptoms include breast tenderness, bloating, headache and pain. Feelings of
and relationships, fatigue and tiredness, difficulty focusing or thinking, food cravings and binge eating, and feeling out of
including suicidality, anxiety and panic attacks, crying, irritability and anger, lack of interest in or attention to activities and r
somatic symptoms include breast tenderness, bloating, headache and pain. Feelings of sadness and despair, even including su
difficulty focusing or thinking, food cravings and binge eating, and feeling out of control are common. Assorted somatic s
attacks, crying, irritability and anger, lack of interest in or attention to activities and relationships, fatigue and tiredness, di
tenderness, bloating, headache and pain. Feelings of sadness and despair, even including suicidality, anxiety and panic attac
food cravings and binge eating, and feeling out of control are common. Assorted somatic symptoms include breast tenderne
lack of interest in or attention to activities and relationships, fatigue and tiredness, difficulty focusing or thinking, food cravi
Feelings of sadness and despair, even including suicidality, anxiety and panic attacks, crying, irritability and anger, lack of int
out of control are common. Assorted somatic symptoms include breast tenderness, bloating, headache and pain. Feelings of
and relationships, fatigue and tiredness, difficulty focusing or thinking, food cravings and binge eating, and feeling out of
including suicidality, anxiety and panic attacks, crying, irritability and anger, lack of interest in or attention to activities and r
somatic symptoms include breast tenderness, bloating, headache and pain. Feelings of sadness and despair, even including su
difficulty focusing or thinking, food cravings and binge eating, and feeling out of control are common. Assorted somatic s
attacks, crying, irritability and anger, lack of interest in or attention to activities and relationships, fatigue and tiredness, di
tenderness, bloating, headache and pain. Feelings of sadness and despair, even including suicidality, anxiety and panic attac
food cravings and binge eating, and feeling out of control are common. Assorted somatic symptoms include breast tenderne
lack of interest in or attention to activities and relationships, fatigue and tiredness, difficulty focusing or thinking, food cravi
Feelings of sadness and despair, even including suicidality, anxiety and panic attacks, crying, irritability and anger, lack of int
out of control are common. Assorted somatic symptoms include breast tenderness, bloating, headache and pain. Feelings of
and relationships, fatigue and tiredness, difficulty focusing or thinking, food cravings and binge eating, and feeling out of
including suicidality, anxiety and panic attacks, crying, irritability and anger, lack of interest in or attention to activities and r
somatic symptoms include breast tenderness, bloating, headache and pain. Feelings of sadness and despair, even including su
difficulty focusing or thinking, food cravings and binge eating, and feeling out of control are common. Assorted somatic s
attacks, crying, irritability and anger, lack of interest in or attention to activities and relationships, fatigue and tiredness, di
tenderness, bloating, headache and pain. Feelings of sadness and despair, even including suicidality, anxiety and panic attac
food cravings and binge eating, and feeling out of control are common. Assorted somatic symptoms include breast tenderne
lack of interest in or attention to activities and relationships, fatigue and tiredness, difficulty focusing or thinking, food cravi
Feelings of sadness and despair, even including suicidality, anxiety and panic attacks, crying, irritability and anger, lack of int
out of control are common. Assorted somatic symptoms include breast tenderness, bloating, headache and pain. Feelings of
and relationships, fatigue and tiredness, difficulty focusing or thinking, food cravings and binge eating, and feeling out of
including suicidality, anxiety and panic attacks, crying, irritability and anger, lack of interest in or attention to activities and r
somatic symptoms include breast tenderness, bloating, headache and pain. Feelings of sadness and despair, even including su
difficulty focusing or thinking, food cravings and binge eating, and feeling out of control are common. Assorted somatic s
attacks, crying, irritability and anger, lack of interest in or attention to activities and relationships, fatigue and tiredness, dif
tenderness, bloating, headache and pain. Feelings of sadness and despair, even including suicidality, anxiety and panic attack
food cravings and binge eating, and feeling out of control are common. Assorted somatic symptoms include breast tenderne
lack of interest in or attention to activities and relationships, fatigue and tiredness, difficulty focusing or thinking, food cravi
Feelings of sadness and despair, even including suicidality, anxiety and panic attacks, crying, irritability and anger, lack of int
out of control are common. Assorted somatic symptoms include breast tenderness, bloating, headache and pain. Feelings of
and relationships, fatigue and tiredness, difficulty focusing or thinking, food cravings and binge eating, and feeling out of c
including suicidality, anxiety and panic attacks, crying, irritability and anger, lack of interest in or attention to activities and r
somatic symptoms include breast tenderness, bloating, headache and pain. Feelings of sadness and despair, even including su
difficulty focusing or thinking, food cravings and binge eating, and feeling out of control are common. Assorted somatic s
attacks, crying, irritability and anger, lack of interest in or attention to activities and relationships, fatigue and tiredness, dif
tenderness, bloating, headache and pain. Feelings of sadness and despair, even including suicidality, anxiety and panic attack
food cravings and binge eating, and feeling out of control are common. Assorted somatic symptoms include breast tenderne
lack of interest in or attention to activities and relationships, fatigue and tiredness, difficulty focusing or thinking, food cravi
Feelings of sadness and despair, even including suicidality, anxiety and panic attacks, crying, irritability and anger, lack of int
out of control are common. Assorted somatic symptoms include breast tenderness, bloating, headache and pain. Feelings of
and relationships, fatigue and tiredness, difficulty focusing or thinking, food cravings and binge eating, and feeling out of c
including suicidality, anxiety and panic attacks, crying, irritability and anger, lack of interest in or attention to activities a

activities and relationships, fatigue and tiredness, difficulty focusing or thinking, food cravings and binge eating, and feeling
even including suicidality, anxiety and panic attacks, crying, irritability and anger, lack of interest in or attention to activities
Assorted somatic symptoms include breast tenderness, bloating, headache and pain. Feelings of sadness and despair, even
nd tiredness, difficulty focusing or thinking, food cravings and binge eating, and feeling out of control are common. Assorted
panic attacks, crying, irritability and anger, lack of interest in or attention to activities and relationships, fatigue and tiredness,
ast tenderness, bloating, headache and pain. Feelings of sadness and despair, even including suicidality, anxiety and panic
inking, food cravings and binge eating, and feeling out of control are common. Assorted somatic symptoms include breast
and anger, lack of interest in or attention to activities and relationships, fatigue and tiredness, difficulty focusing or thinking,
and pain. Feelings of sadness and despair, even including suicidality, anxiety and panic attacks, crying, irritability and anger,
and feeling out of control are common. Assorted somatic symptoms include breast tenderness, bloating, headache and pain.
activities and relationships, fatigue and tiredness, difficulty focusing or thinking, food cravings and binge eating, and feeling
even including suicidality, anxiety and panic attacks, crying, irritability and anger, lack of interest in or attention to activities
Assorted somatic symptoms include breast tenderness, bloating, headache and pain. Feelings of sadness and despair, even
nd tiredness, difficulty focusing or thinking, food cravings and binge eating, and feeling out of control are common. Assorted
panic attacks, crying, irritability and anger, lack of interest in or attention to activities and relationships, fatigue and tiredness,
east tenderness, bloating, headache and pain. Feelings of sadness and despair, even including suicidality, anxiety and panic
inking, food cravings and binge eating, and feeling out of control are common. Assorted somatic symptoms include breast
and anger, lack of interest in or attention to activities and relationships, fatigue and tiredness, difficulty focusing or thinking,
and pain. Feelings of sadness and despair, even including suicidality, anxiety and panic attacks, crying, irritability and anger,
and feeling out of control are common. Assorted somatic symptoms include breast tenderness, bloating, headache and pain.
activities and relationships, fatigue and tiredness, difficulty focusing or thinking, food cravings and binge eating, and feeling
even including suicidality, anxiety and panic attacks, crying, irritability and anger, lack of interest in or attention to activities
Assorted somatic symptoms include breast tenderness, bloating, headache and pain. Feelings of sadness and despair, even
nd tiredness, difficulty focusing or thinking, food cravings and binge eating, and feeling out of control are common. Assorted
panic attacks, crying, irritability and anger, lack of interest in or attention to activities and relationships, fatigue and tiredness,
east tenderness, bloating, headache and pain. Feelings of sadness and despair, even including suicidality, anxiety and panic
inking, food cravings and binge eating, and feeling out of control are common. Assorted somatic symptoms include breast
and anger, lack of interest in or attention to activities and relationships, fatigue and tiredness, difficulty focusing or thinking,
and pain. Feelings of sadness and despair, even including suicidality, anxiety and panic attacks, crying, irritability and anger,
and feeling out of control are common. Assorted somatic symptoms include breast tenderness, bloating, headache and pain.
activities and relationships, fatigue and tiredness, difficulty focusing or thinking, food cravings and binge eating, and feeling
even including suicidality, anxiety and panic attacks, crying, irritability and anger, lack of interest in or attention to activities
Assorted somatic symptoms include breast tenderness, bloating, headache and pain. Feelings of sadness and despair, even
nd tiredness, difficulty focusing or thinking, food cravings and binge eating, and feeling out of control are common. Assorted
panic attacks, crying, irritability and anger, lack of interest in or attention to activities and relationships, fatigue and tiredness,
east tenderness, bloating, headache and pain. Feelings of sadness and despair, even including suicidality, anxiety and panic
inking, food cravings and binge eating, and feeling out of control are common. Assorted somatic symptoms include breast
and anger, lack of interest in or attention to activities and relationships, fatigue and tiredness, difficulty focusing or thinking,
and pain. Feelings of sadness and despair, even including suicidality, anxiety and panic attacks, crying, irritability and anger,
and feeling out of control are common. Assorted somatic symptoms include breast tenderness, bloating, headache and pain.
activities and relationships, fatigue and tiredness, difficulty focusing or thinking, food cravings and binge eating, and feeling
even including suicidality, anxiety and panic attacks, crying, irritability and anger, lack of interest in or attention to activities
Assorted somatic symptoms include breast tenderness, bloating, headache and pain. Feelings of sadness and despair, even
nd tiredness, difficulty focusing or thinking, food cravings and binge eating, and feeling out of control are common. Assorted
panic attacks, crying, irritability and anger, lack of interest in or attention to activities and relationships, fatigue and tiredness,
east tenderness, bloating, headache and pain. Feelings of sadness and despair, even including suicidality, anxiety and panic
inking, food cravings and binge eating, and feeling out of control are common. Assorted somatic symptoms include breast
and anger, lack of interest in or attention to activities and rela or 10 years, spent menstruating g or thinking,
and pain. Feelings of sadness and despair, even including sui llity and anger,
and feeling out of control are common. Assorted somatic symptoms include breast tenderness, bloating, headache and pain.
activities and relationships, fatigue and tiredness, difficulty focusing or thinking, food cravings and binge eating, and feeling
even including suicidality, anxiety and panic attacks, crying, irritability and anger, lack of interest in or attention to activities
Assorted somatic symptoms include breast tenderness, bloating, headache and pain. Feelings of sadness and despair, even
nd tiredness, difficulty focusing or thinking, food cravings and binge eating, and feeling out of control are common. Assorted
panic attacks, crying, irritability and anger, lack of interest in or attention to activities and relationships, fatigue and tiredness,
east tenderness, bloating, headache and pain. Feelings of sadness and despair, even including suicidality, anxiety and panic
inking, food cravings and binge eating, and feeling out of control are common. Assorted somatic symptoms include breast
and anger, lack of interest in or attention to activities and relationships, fatigue and tiredness, difficulty focusing or thinking,
and pain. Feelings of sadness and despair, even including suicidality, anxiety and panic attacks, crying, irritability and anger,
and feeling out of control are common. Assorted somatic symptoms include breast tenderness, bloating, headache and pain.
activities and relationships, fatigue and tiredness, difficulty focusing or thinking, food cravings and binge eating, and feeling
even including suicidality, anxiety and panic attacks, crying, irritability and anger, lack of interest in or attention to activities
Assorted somatic symptoms include breast tenderness, bloating, headache and pain. Feelings of sadness and despair, even
igue and tiredness, difficulty focusing or thinking, food cravings and binge eating, and feeling out of control are common.

when do I need to

"most people call an ambulance after experiencing chest pain for five minutes"

self-portrait of the patient as an emergency diabetic ketoacidosis

dry mouth, excessive thirst and urination,
high blood glucose levels, and high ketone
levels. As ketoacidosis progresses, you may
have fatigue; flushed or try skin; abdominal
pain, nausea, or vomiting; short, deep
breaths, confusion; and a fruity odour on
your breath

dry mouth, excessive thirst and urination,
high blood glucose levels, and high ketone
levels. As ketoacidosis progresses, you may
have fatigue; flushed or dry skin; abdominal
pain, nausea, or vomiting; short, deep
breaths, confusion; and a fruity odour on
your breath

dry mouth, excessive thirst and urination,
high blood glucose levels, and high ketone
levels. As ketoacidosis progresses, you may
have fatigue; flushed or try skin; abdominal
pain, nausea, or vomiting; short, deep
breaths, confusion; and a fruity odour on
your breath

the lucky ones

In Canada, total health care costs attributed to diabetes are 15.36 billion dollars over ten years.

The management and prevention of diabetes remains a health priority.

"my chest pain and
breathing problems
haven't stopped"

"I threw up after the CT"

*"I'm trying not to think of the
implications of being twenty-seven
with blood clots in my lungs"*

"my chest pain
is back"

"they went 1.5cm in at one point, and
through my hand"

"but it's not a
blood clot"

"they took five vials.
usually my blood stops
flowing at three."

"they couldn't find my
veins. I'm all bruised
everywhere. PICC line"

"ultrasound for a vein"

"the PICC line is
scary"

"it's not a heart attack or a blood clot"

"I haven't been able to breathe properly in a month"

"they sent me home
with a blood thinner
shot"

"I'm going to the
emergency room"

Part 3: disability

to sit in an exit row

to sit in an exit row:
you must be willing to save those you love or
a plane full of strangers who have been told
not to help you with your oxygen mask or
heavy baggage, even when you tell them your mother
never says sorry either, or that after thirty years
your father takes so much insulin even
the 8 mm's don't go deep enough

to sit in an exit row you must let go
of the fear of death and the refusal to die
or the fact that there could be enough test strips
to go around if the men in suits wanted it
you'll be asked to go quietly
even though the plane will not go quietly
because people like you know
to let the screaming go on inside
like it does at the pharmacy or family dinner
when it's your fault the Plan B doesn't work
and it is your fault for getting fat
or failing the neurologists' tests
or crying when your doctor quits and doesn't tell you about it

exit rows are for people with lives worth living
not you and your tarnished reflexes
your bag of pills of extra days they check at security
to ensure that no one will die from the things that keep you alive
because neither of your insurances will cover it
the pads of your fingers bludgeoned
by the morning finger sticks
and your heart, pumping blood cells with thorns round their necks
asking to be freed as you kiss your pancreas awake

to sit in an exit row, you must be willing to live past eighteen
or at least twelve, if accompanied by a guardian, you must
be willing to write poems in French and English, fuck Gujarati
to see the sun and sky the day you die
in a plane crash, the way no one expects it
you must be willing to evacuate from
your life and your body

and if between the time of booking and journey
the above requirements cannot be met
you may ask for a refund on the continuous glucose monitors or fasting
glucose tests or the emergency glucose pills or the SGLT2 inhibitors or
the appetite suppressants or the medical tape pulling your hair or the
butterfly needles entering your veins downstream from tourniquets tied
too tight for the vial after vial of blood that they will never give back

and when they ask if you accept that you must be willing to die
so that everyone else goes on having a good time
you can finally say *I'm used to it.*

the latest news says Diet Coke causes cancer

and it's a miracle, you think, that this news breaks at all, too late for your waistline, that this news gets to the public the way Big Coke gets New Coke out of the public, and how did the word on Diet Coke get out?

is Big Coke playing the long game, producing a movie on Big Cola twenty years from now when Warner Bros. gets bought by the Big Coke Brothers, and the only moviegoers in twenty years will be the moms who survived the cancer and their daughters, who survived their moms

their shelves the last wreckage of trends to keep you thinner than the round belly of a glass bottle of Coca-Cola, *mhhhhm ahhhhh*

Diet Coke Lets You Have Your Cake and Eat It Too you know, we knew, we knew that there are worse ways to die than with three silver crushed aluminium cans over our eyes sealing

our mouth shut to be popped over a cold river made of melting polar ice to bring us home.

no evidence of pulmonary embolism

A three-month pneumonia, followed by a six-month recovery. Words don't taste the same because they sit for longer in my mouth. For days I slept in batches, woken by the cracking of my own lungs. I performed on my knees to a microphone that did not heal me. I couldn't breathe. I couldn't breathe, for weeks, for months, for for for—is it permanent now? Poems don't taste the same, can't be swallowed. They take everything out of me. I tire within moments. I have to speak so slowly that I lose my own train of thought. I am trapped in my own esophagus. I can't take these lungs anywhere anymore.

in the aftermath of the poisoned lung, which did not heal and does not get better

who am I now that disease has turned my lungs to curled leaves and ash, cracked bark, the smell of bleeding brown into the black earth after a forest fire, struggling under the heat of a naked sun, if I had known that I would one day take my last full exhale before Christmas I would have spent it saying your name, I would have lain on the bed like a tree falls on the dirt, and prayed to the universe to find my roots again, and it's been ten months since the doctor told me it would be all right, and still there are no pine cones here, no seeds of regrowth, the cracked breath breathes no fire, I do not rise, I am innumerable tunnels abandoned by the ants, the air is trapped in my collapse, my lungs, oh my lungs, how the bacteria made a feast in your wake, how I came to know you in farewell, I haven't held my breath since Halloween, haven't screamed or panicked, run down the hill to the river, since the X-rays came back clean, some days I think I imagined it, the bed and its gravity, the way my words tasted like a rock slide when they left my mouth, the weeks when I weighed as much as a small moon, looked into the mirror and saw only craters, there are days I woke in the cold and knew I would never get better, never sing off-key and bloated again, I've had to reacquaint myself with a microphone that bends like a serpent's coil around my throat, and some might call it a miracle to survive the fear of death as well as death itself, no one wants to know how much I wanted to die and how much I wanted to live in equal measure, how I imagined collapsing in Kensington Market where only the tar and snow would embalm me, you have no idea how much of a person lives inside their body until their body tries to escape, who am I now that my lungs speak the same language as the oil paints, they know nothing of being transparent or breathable, nothing of cotton pyjamas on the clothesline or wind in the sharp grass, nothing of a prairie storm chasing the bees, some days I wake and I forget that I am not a childhood bedroom or a dresser, places filled with space to store my memories of the days when I could inhale without drowning.

i'll never be hungry again

Another visit to the emergency room, and thank god I'm not wasting their time after all. Ketoacidosis but we're not sure why, certainly I'm fat enough to be a Type 2 diabetic, and everyone I will tell afterward is sure to correct me when I say that the doctors suspect Type 1 from the DKA. Who's the expert here? The sugar has addled my brain, the same as the lack of serotonin and the norepinephrine that dances in and out. My receptors are revolving doors, my cells coated in spikes, my A1C above the legal limit, and my boyfriend warns me not to eat. Sure. I wasn't hungry anyway. I'll never be hungry again.

when i learn that I am Disabled

I am getting through five days of paranoid anxiety
through my brain not working the way it is supposed to

     did you know that disability is a social construct?

that the majority define what it means to thrive
that lack is problematized as weakness
that in an accepting society we are all a little disabled
but no one is told they are less
no one is left wanting more

and when my brain does not work the way it's supposed to
     it's okay

because we're all worth our weight in good days
and my good days are not worth less than your good days
that you having more good days doesn't make you
     more good
     or deserving of more days

when I google

VAMPIRES

I am not looking for a way to live forever
I am looking for a way to be remembered for something more than my
body

if a diabetic is bitten at the neck and drained, does her pancreas get
immortalized too?
what about my flimsy serotonin receptors?
or my elevated adrenalin?

does my heart still want to beat too fast, or is it stuck not beating for
anything at all?

when I google

COVID SYMPTOMS

for the sixtieth time in four hundred days,
I am not looking for a reason to save myself
I am looking for a way to save others from the pharmacy counters that
take too long
or the insurance paperwork that asks too much
the pills you can split by hand
or the big ones you swallow whole
I am looking for ways to reassure myself that there is hope

when I google

DISABILITY

the Government of Canada says *Disability Benefits include disability
pensions and children's benefits, savings plans, and a gasoline tax refund
program*

and I guess that does not sound so bad when it's called a benefit

when I learn I am disabled, I inject insulin invented a hundred years ago
into the same thighs I cut open at sixteen under the fog of manic
depression

I fight the ache of my ovaries
the beast behind breasts that bashes the gate of my rib cage
I fight the rush of blood to my sides as I beg never to become a woman
again

I say no to the birth control pills because being fat is a liability
I say yes to the IUD that renders me crippled for two weeks, unable to
move anything below my pelvis
I say no to the SSRIs that try to kill me
I say yes to the antipsychotics that try to stop me from killing me

I go outside.

being *disabled* means
I am no longer a series of questions in an emergency room
a misplaced PICC line or an X-rayed lung that proves the diagnosis wrong

and I know that knowing something is wrong
is better than knowing nothing at all
better than living in anger or fear of sudden death

because people like me die sometimes and no one cares

but I am lucky that when I die I will notice
I will feel a sigh of relief, I will know that I did my best, and if it wasn't
enough, it isn't my fault
that I tried, that trying when your body fails is a gift to yourself

I am not afraid to die, after all
I am afraid of who I might fail to be if I live in fear of death

when I google

WAYS TO SAY I LOVE YOU WITHOUT SAYING I LOVE YOU

I know that going to bed, and waking up,
is one of them.

Staples closes at 5 p.m. and so I am rushing and

I learn they make 0.9mm lead pencils now
twenty years too late for the growth spurt
that ballooned my bending hands
into the white of the erasers I'm holding

and I haven't used a mechanical pencil in ten years since becoming a
"poet"
fingers different, not so much the supple stem of a leaf
more HB cramped in wood
slow as time ages me

arthritis or atrophy, whatever Google tells me to call it

I have enough money to buy what I wanted at twelve and what I can at
thirty-one
wonder if they make crayons in grown-up colours
like navy instead of blue,
blush instead of pink,
blue-black instead of

that one midnight when we didn't rush but ended up in the ER again
to hear the latest of the crumbling diagnoses spilling out of my body
like broken lead from my backpack

Crayola makes scented crayons in packs of twelve
how many poems could I write in raspberry, dandelion, clean laundry

they sell everything now

I could be anyone, burn a new me into my skin like hot glue
and I wonder if the woman working at Staples
which is closing at 5 p.m. knows
as she restocks the 0.9mm Z-Grips
and the 0.7mm Hilroys

and the 0.5mm Pentels

and all of their plastic is in her hands, pressed against her chest,
condensing as she breathes

and all of my pens are unerasable

because I see the plastic in her arm too
a hard grey rectangle with the word Dexcom
in the vicinity of her name tag

I don't need introductions or advice for quick-drying gel pens

and I ask her if they make a 1mm mechanical pencil and she says no,
there's only a 2mm with the compasses and rulers and drafting papers

and I don't know how to calculate surface area for diabetes
when it's bigger than the 3cm of her glucose monitor
the 0.4mm needle that enters the interstitial fluid beneath her skin
that was easy, soft and flexible as a kitten's whisker

insertion a sharp click like my Spacemaker pencil case
pushing $149.88 into place
branding a person as prescriptions
branding blood as benefits
branding the $14.93 per hour she makes as an opportunity cost

I want to say hello like I say hello to the people
in the waiting rooms of endocrinology, rheumatology

but my tongue is off-brand glue and cheap pink rubber
and all I whisper is *thank you, thank you, thank you*
as faint as graphite on lined paper

second base in assemblage theory is just first base squared

knotting our adipose tissue until my inflammation causes your back pain, your neck pain, your thumb pain
from carrying two of our bodies as one body

I let you gather in me like a Christmas party, my favourite holiday, marry you on Christmas Day if I could, Sufjan Stevens in the background as the lights struggle to stay lit on the Christmas tree, and it would be three days before your birthday, and six days before your mum's, and one week before school starts again

and the thing she loves most in the world is you, and the thing I love most in the world is us, so she loves me too, and she's a part of us because she loves you

and we are a body that joins in heat and then splits with separate blankets in a queen-size bed

and we are a unified and overlapping desire, an embodied wanting, a tongue or two in two or more places, looking for a nourishing of a hunger we can't name when we feel it, we are extending our time and place on Earth through the pink silicone and water-based combinations, we are fingers in dykes stemming an inevitable sweeping off our feet

we throw out our toenails at the same time since you cut all nineteen

my body was an organ once, a sea cucumber of a single opening with two ends

you were the ocean filtering through me

our body knows that drifting in a current and giving in to sway is a type of longing to escape who the world wants us to be, overlapping in one place forever, in one body of the ocean of everywhere and every going, I'd rather drink the water you touched with the lips I went numb against in my car where the dyed cow leather met our raised shirts and I felt holy, like you believed in me, like I was the only god for you

what if you were the problem

sleeping off the Ativan while I worked
pushing away the Metamucil and the iron
throwing up your meds after dinner and
fainting in the heat of the shower before noon

what if it was you on the mattress
that we put in the living room
so we could be together while the TV played
wishing for the room to stop spiralling
like water down the slides at *our* mall

what if it was your lungs that had audibly cracked beneath the weight
of colonies and trees and their branches growing fruit in your alveoli
or you at the podiatrist getting measured for $800 inserts while I bought
Dunk Lows
what if it was your feet that swelled so bad they ripened like Tommy Atkins
mangoes
and your back that bent with the weight of your stomach
that puffed out like a sigh from your body

what if it was you on that bed that time and the next
you who was too tired to eat or walk or fuck
you with the screens and the tubes and the nurses
you getting the chest X-rays and the ultrasounds and the CTs
you with the electricity splashing through your nerves
so that we knew you could still feel me when we touched

what if it was you, what if it was you, what if it was you
who I'd been waiting for my whole life
who I would have done anything improbable for
like praying or buying a centrifuge or getting a medical degree
what if it was you in my arms
when we wake together after the show
where I held your hand at the microphone in the mirror
and asked them
to take me instead

let me be of no use

let me be of no use
to you or your affairs,
your loved ones, your life insurance, your benefits,
your cupholders, your passenger seat

I will leave the cupboards open
two inches of every drawer
and ants will grow in the crumbs
and leftovers will go bad in the fridge
I will forget to replace the toilet paper

let me be of no use
when the fitted sheet comes undone
and we end up on the blasphemy of a bare mattress
with only the old yellow pillows to keep us cool

and when the unfinished bottles of Coke Zero start to line the counter
and the toothpaste is nearly empty
and the new TV remote falls behind the headboard
and every pair of Crocs I own remains in the entryway
let me be of no use

in the carrying and the laundering of things, the stack of unopened
mail, the oil change, the credit score, the vacuuming, the lint and the
lint rolling, the wringing, the burning stove

let me be of no use
            to productivity, to society, to orienteering, mountaineering
            snow clearing, balcony sweeping, road-trip navigating

let me be of no use
in comprehending
how much you love me

not in spite of all that I can't and won't be
but because of it, because of the way you like it
and let it be of no use to apologize or ask forgiveness
for wanting and holding on to the joy you find
in taking care of me

the body without organs,
in response to Deleuze and Guattari

a map reinforces itself
so go forward with no map
go forward toward your body without knowing what a body has to be

and if I could choose my body I'd let go of everything but my heart
I'd become a part of your body
I'd move into a bedroom next to stars and never worry about falling asleep
or waking up in my body

if my body could speak it would ask you to listen
to forget the instructions to my body
to make it up like a child makes up the dinosaur's cry

and maybe wanting to hear the dinosaurs again is a type of body
for what is desire if not an assembly within the space I call my body

and they say no mathematician can prove a body that has no bounds
yet possibility is the foundation of all mathematical bodies

maybe philosophy is just a way for grief to escape a body and take everyone
with it

maybe thinking of bodies is all wrong
maybe calling them bodies is too much
maybe your thoughts of me are a body
and without all our tangling organs we get to be one body

I am a treble clef's body catching your sharps in my hands
I am a score and you are my epiphany
we get coffee and I become a coffee shop
my body a conversation I can't tune out
my body a fleeting connection

my body a future that repeats itself
like my coffee with cream repeats itself
is my body more last week than it is next week
is my coffee a body if the sugar can't be recrystallized
is tasting something sweet only once a type of body
is the water in your bottle a body
or is it part of a body you will return to when you die?
is death a type of body
and if it is, then why are the philosophers always thirsty?
will my body remember this week at the end of its last week?
what is a body if your body falters often, if repetition and routine are a part
of your body?

am I a body made machine to work itself to grease
inflamed joint and burning jaw

is my body is an instrument I can keep?

one I can take home and play until the neighbours sing too
and is the sound my body makes still part of my body if no one wants to
hear it?

or is wanting to be heard enough to make me human?
to make me a human in a human body, is it enough
to make my life worth saving
if it is saved inside of my body?

ode to pneumonia

tell me one day I'll look back at that bed above Bloor Street
and recall the way my body found solace in the radiator
that sludged-over, slick rib cage
a survivor of the eviction that emptied the kitchen of coffee filters and
honey

both of us rattling out a dying breath of warmth in a room of cold silence
our parallel pain, our creaking airways, our attempts at giving up, all
ignored by our bones
the insistent metallic taste of blood in my mouth
proof of my body's wilfulness and shamelessness, proof of its unsexy
mouth breathing
we infest ourselves with germs and hope

and pray

*there is a small focus of consolidation projected over the right lower lung
zone involving an area measuring 4.1cm*

tell me, do you believe that I fell in love that day? the colony in my lungs
seeded something so awful that I gave up my ego, my oxygen, my insides,
my pride, in the blur of eyes too sore for glasses, a body too weak to sit
up, a throat pulling apart at the seams like ripped fingernails. that in
those moments of grief I faced a vastness, an expanse within myself that
left no bounds for the thing I grew there. from the way he begged the
convenience store to sell a roll of toilet paper after midnight, the bubble
tea he walked back in the wind, do you believe in the love that grew from
the refilling cup of tea, and the extra blankets, and the way he looked at
me on that bed with my hair bleached and dry after our $70 plane over
and still said *I want you I want you I want you*

*difficult to visualize on the lateral radiograph. probable right lower lobe
pneumonia*

tell me, do you believe there is a new kind of wanting out there, one they didn't show me in the books and magazines, or X-rays, that comes from wanting someone so much you cannot see them as what they could be, or what they were, only as what they are when they are with you, tell me, tell me, tell me

heart size is normal. the left lung is clear. radiographic follow-up is recommended until resolution

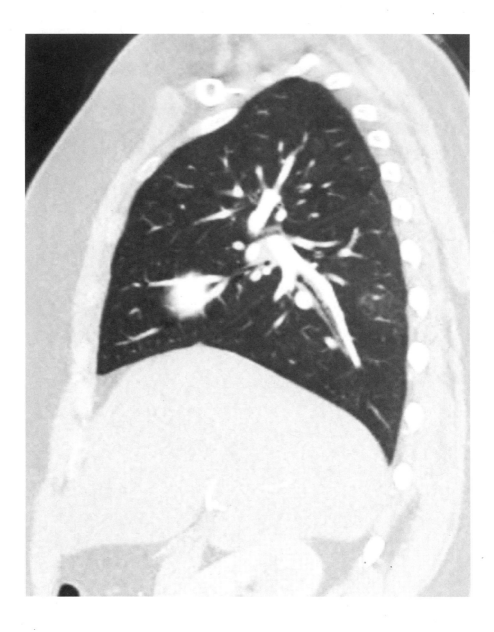

give me my cyborg eyes
after Jasbir Puar and Donna Haraway

I would say the disabled body is the most possible

because it takes being told what you cannot do
to dream of new ways that you can

it takes living at the edges of acceptability
to accept a billion new takes on living
for who knows how to define the world we need
more than the people who need it?

who knows what sorrow can spring more than those who sing it?

the boundary of what *we* know is different
than of those who live lives with working toes and eyes
who can still walk and smile around us

for those who live at the margins of what society wants
know that wanting is not enough

and if it takes being near death to value each second I spend living my life
then I'll risk it

      every day
      in every universe

its fraughtful realities, scars and missing legs and plastic hearts and
chemically healed lacerations

give me my cyborg eyes
give me my cyborg ribs
give me my cyborg tongue

the future depends on my cyborg thighs and cyborg lungs

because it will take a million sick bodies to find the cures and contagions
that will save us

> the lab rats get worse before they get better
> and all lab rats are worth saving as they huddle together

the future depends on redefining what it means to be human
> because being human alone won't free us

and we're the only beings I've met with this capacity for imagination
so I want you to pick new eyes, new hearts, new lungs

I'd rather be a cyborg than a finite and limited body
I'd rather be an IV drip and walking stick than two fast-moving feet trying
to be somebody
I'd rather be a place that holds your feelings
an object of desire
> or a site of possibility

of what is, and what comes next

I want to be disabled in every universe, with you
> more than I want to be remembered for something
> its true.

so give me cyborg eyes
give me my cyborg eyes
give me my cyborg eyes

and look around you now: my disabled dreams arc infinite.

"We need the poets to imagine for us. The duty of Heaven-making should be attached to the office of the Poet Laureate. Indeed it is to the poets that we turn."

—Virginia Woolf, "On Being Ill"

This edition is limited to one numbered copy, signed by the author and not for sale. this type has been set by the author. this type has been set in blood and needles, in pinpricks of flesh, in a small wound on a large thigh, a dark canvas of pigment and shame. this type is a morning injection and a midnight snack, this type is a disease passed on from the author's ancestors, this type is for the author who keeps a juice box in every room, who leaves class twice to vomit or expel breakfast, these pages are a layer cake of blame thrown at a girl on the playground, this author is a girl on the playground throwing blame around, this type of author is made of AB+ but her platelets are useless with all that so-called deficiency, this author is the type to check the boxes and take the money, this author has been told there is no cure, this author is made up of stories that break skin, stories that soak, and stain, and cut her open like her body cuts open her red blood cells at the tiniest wound, at the smallest of cancers, at the slightest touch. this edition of the author is a type of fleeting, a type of numbering, like diabetes II or alpha thalassemia or a ferritin of 4, and is not for sale, yet *fin*

Acknowledgments

I want to acknowledge the infallible support of the Edmonton Arts Council and the support of Alberta Foundation for the Arts during early drafts of the manuscript. This project was rejected by the Canada Council for the Arts two separate times.

Select poems in this book have appeared in previous publications, including *Briarpatch*, *filling Station*, *Arc Poetry Magazine* and in my chapbook *NOT A DISORDER* from Gap Riot Press.

Portions of this book have also appeared in my short film, *a fate worse than death*, which comprised part of my master of arts thesis at Queen's University. I owe a deep debt to Dr. Thomas Abrams, who curated a syllabus in disability studies that changed my life. Through the ongoing COVID-19 pandemic, I also came to know the work of Dr. Travis Chi Wing Lau, Dr. Jasbir Puar, Dr. Donna Haraway, and the many incredible disabled authors at Arsenal Pulp Press, including Leah Lakshmi Piepzna-Samarasinha and the collective work of Sins Invalid. My editor, Natalie Wee, has an attention to poetic rigour that I will continue to learn from.

A show called *a fate worse than death* debuted over three nights in 2023 at the Nextfest Mainstage, allowing me to take space in the Lorne Cardinal Theatre for an entire hour of solo poetry and music (clumsily, with many technical issues and a low glycemic episode).

I also want to thank Jordan Abel for being the first to see the potential in this inquiry and for his many reference letters for grants, graduate schools, scholarships, jobs, and awards that followed and continue to follow (sorry). All of these things allowed me to create the work and recreate it with intention and love.

And to Matthew, my intellectual ally / fiancé / partner, I am sorry I don't update any of my drivers and then cry about it until you fix it. I love you.

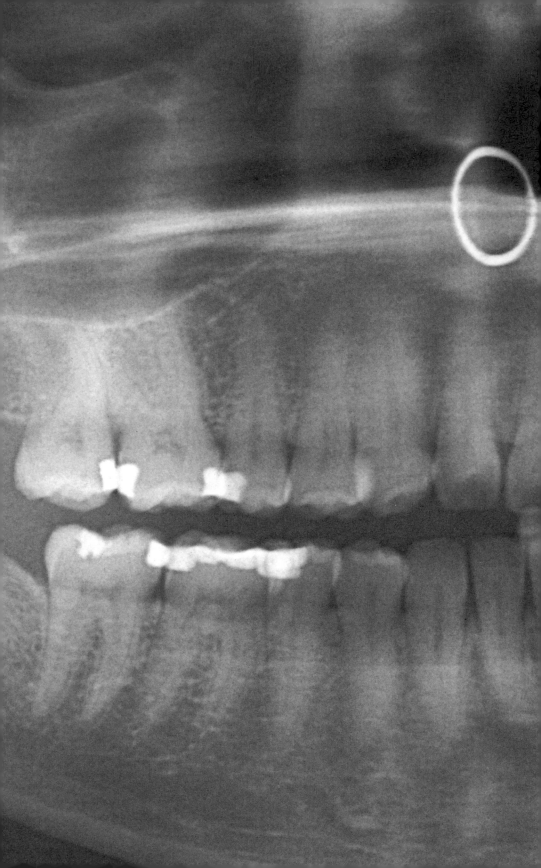

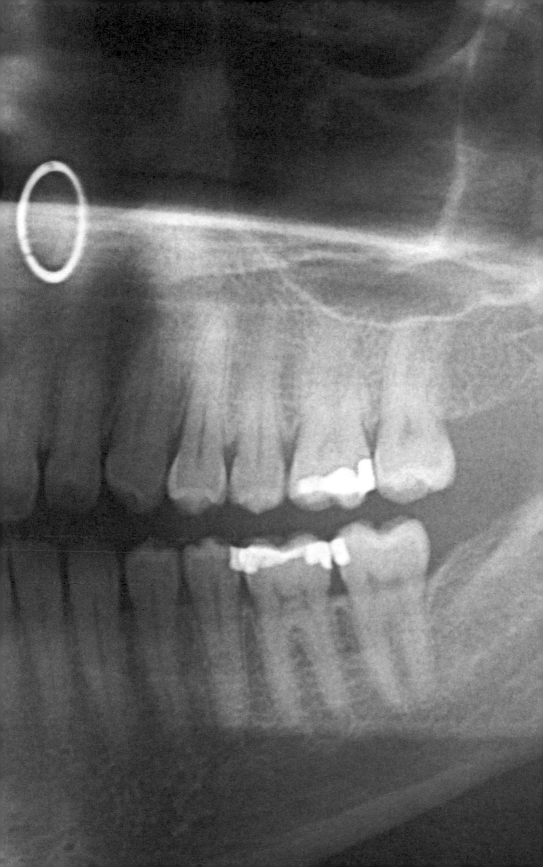

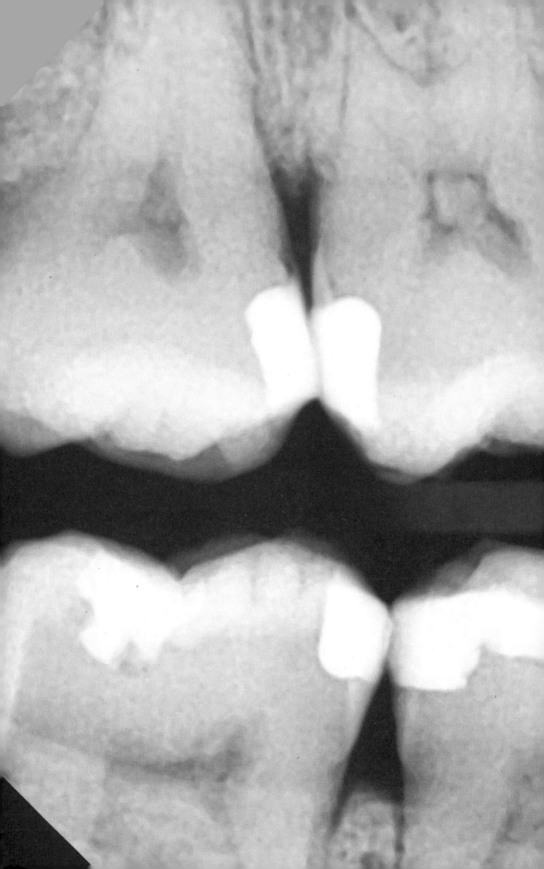

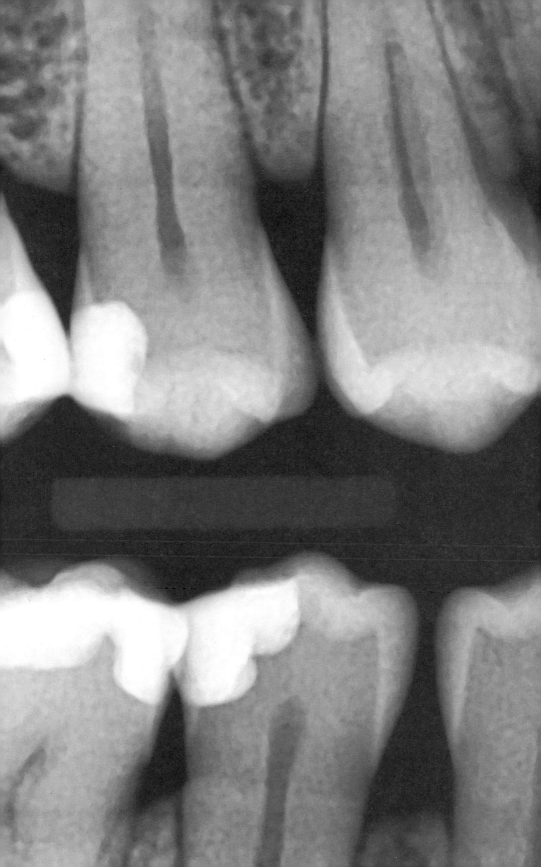

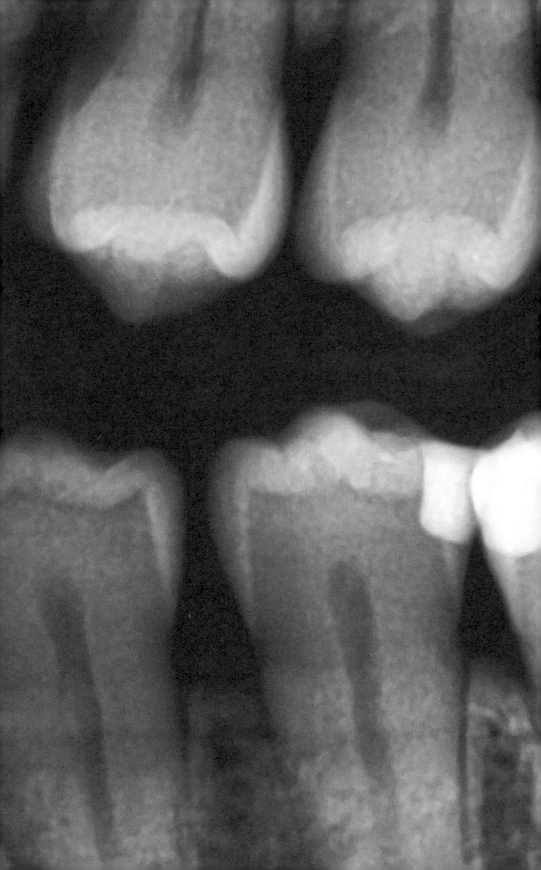

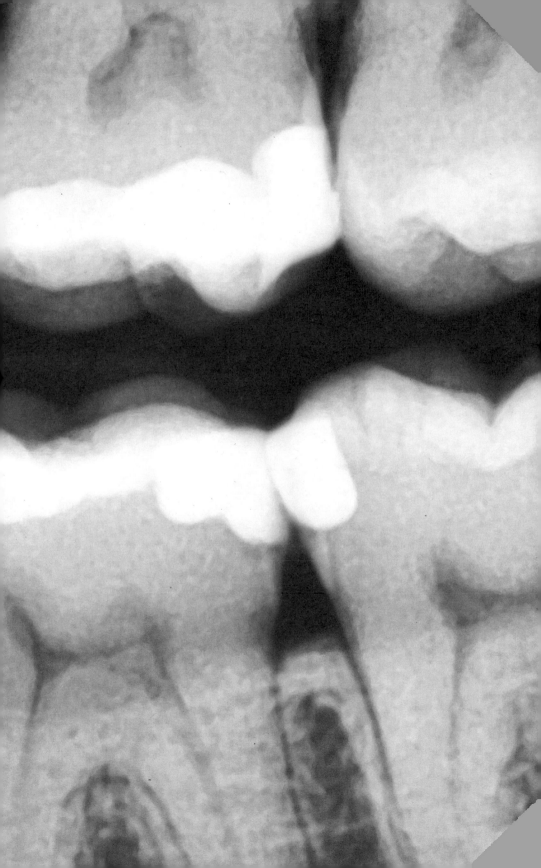

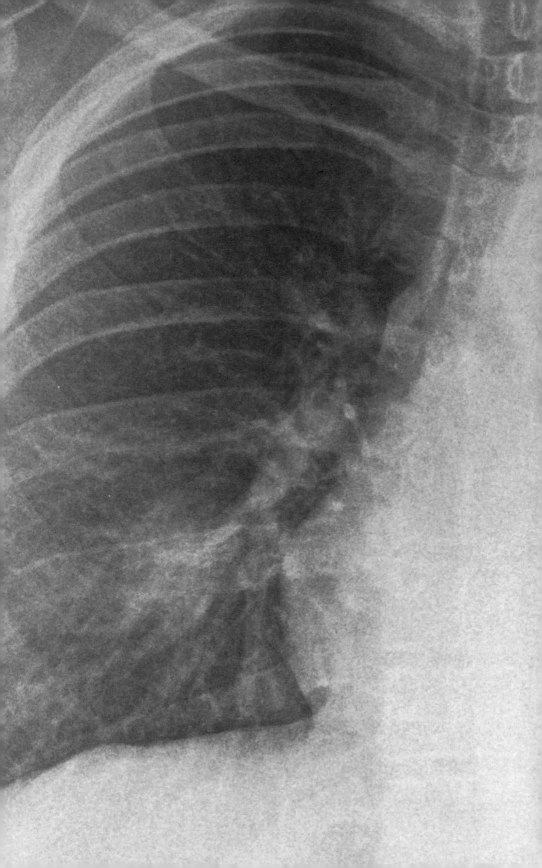

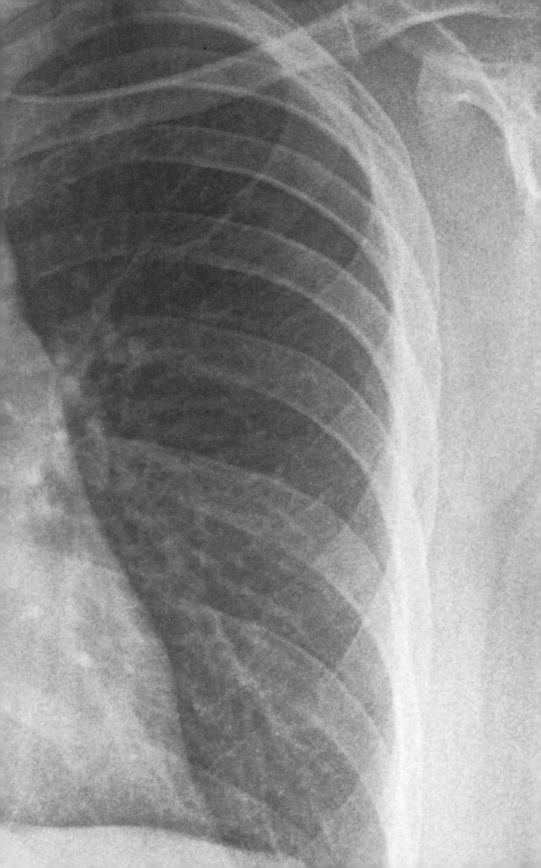

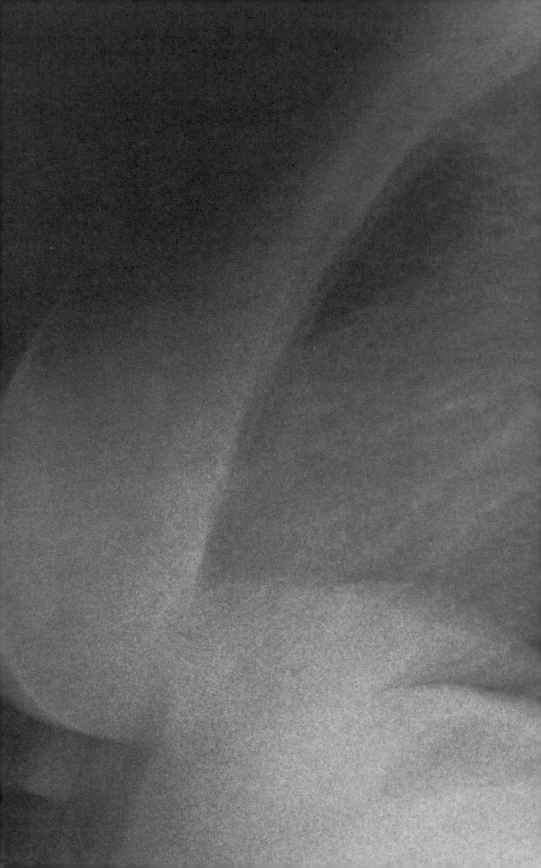

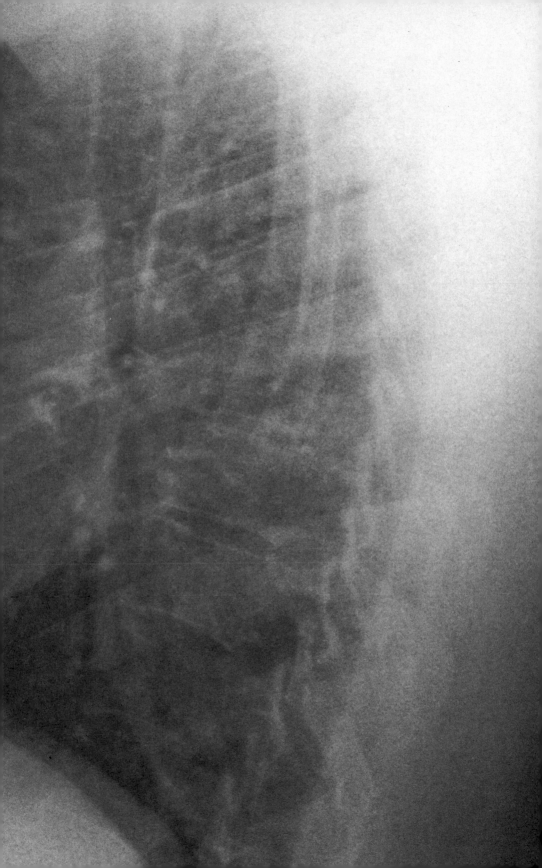

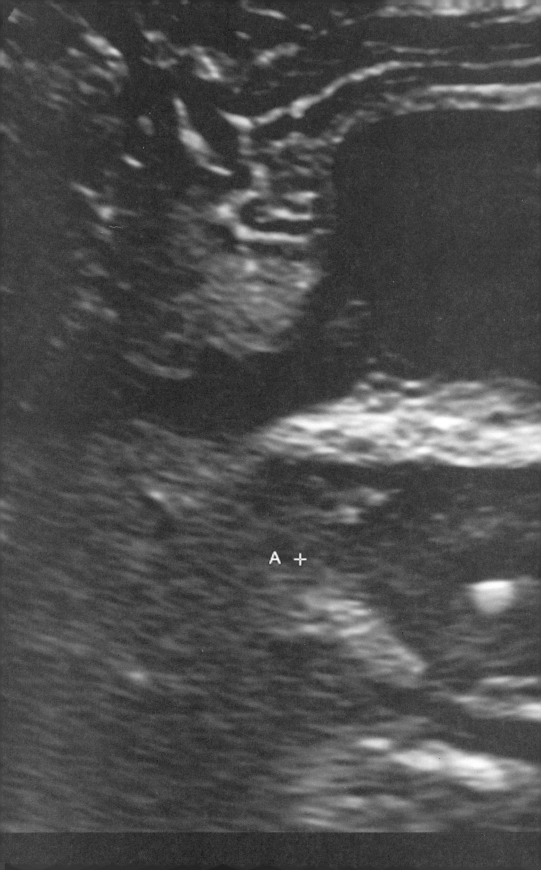

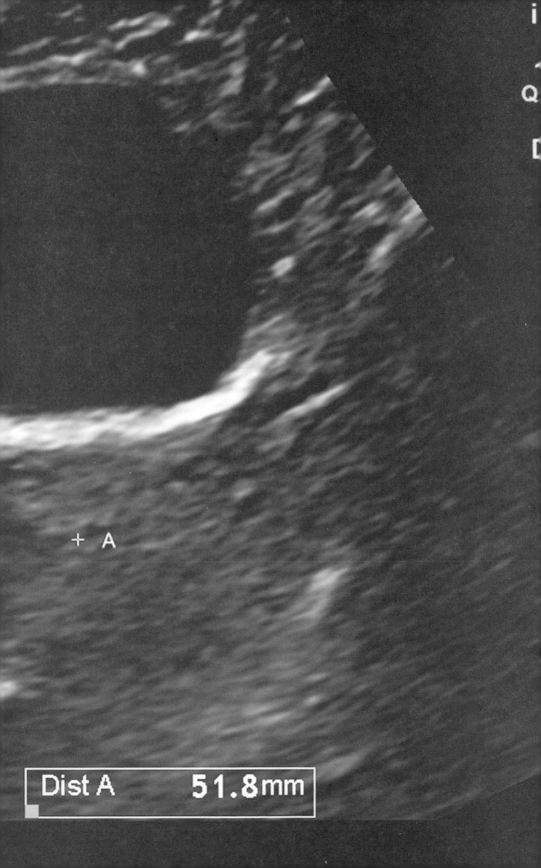

+ A

Dist A   51.8mm

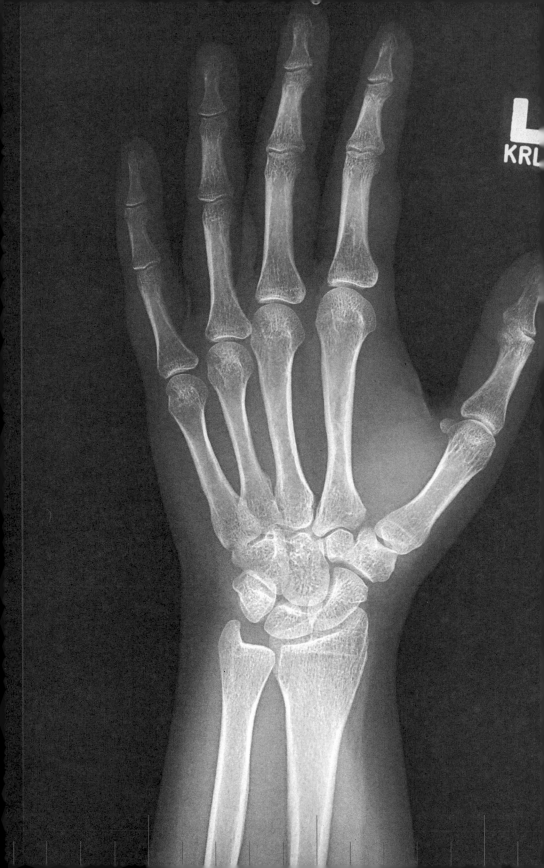

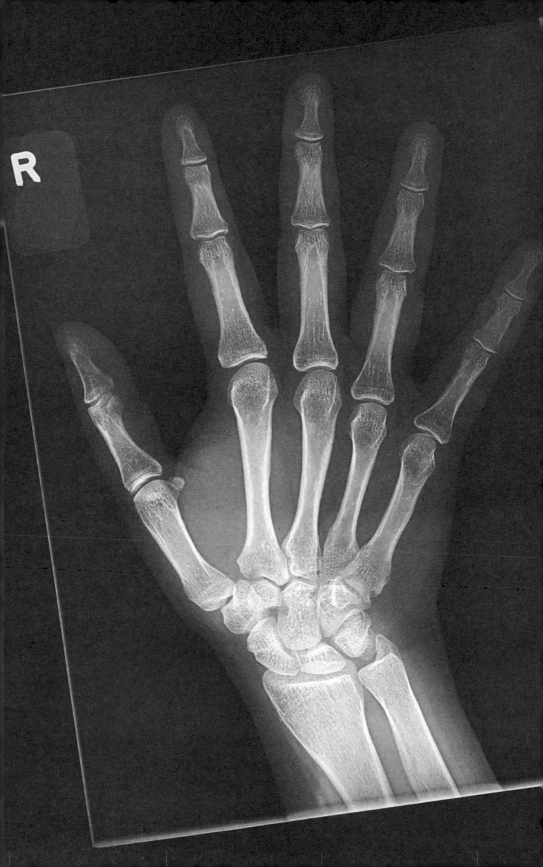

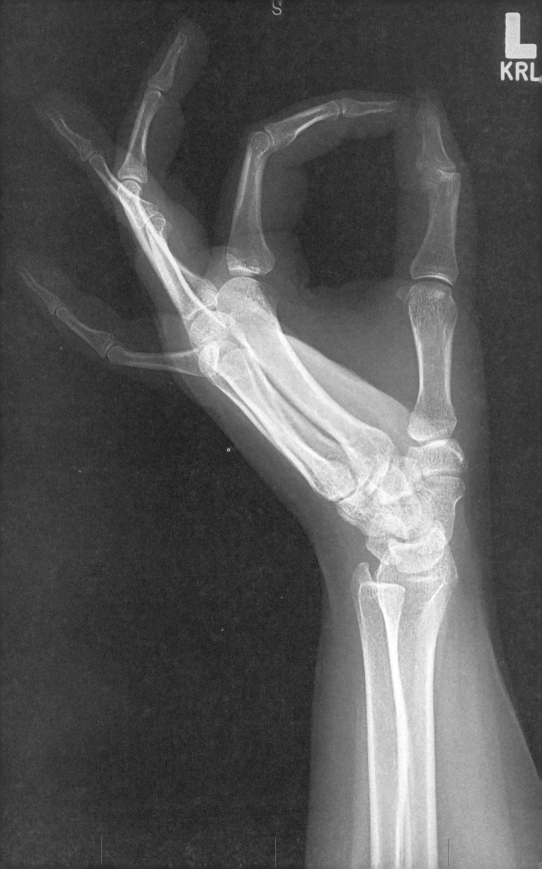

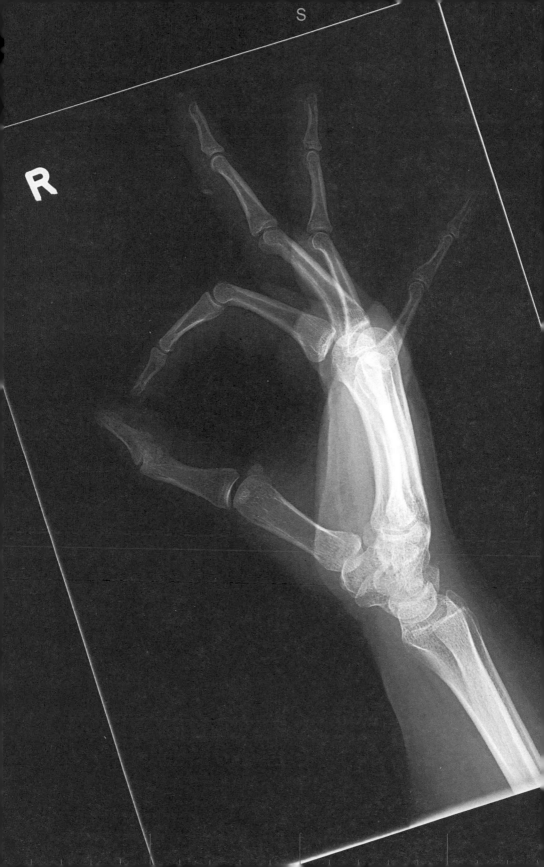

Nisha Patel is a Poet Laureate Emeritus of the City of
Edmonton. An award-winning disabled and queer artist,
she is a Canadian Individual Poetry Slam champion and
holds a master of arts in cultural studies from Queen's
University. Her debut poetry collection, *Coconut*, is
out with NeWest Press, alongside her latest chapbooks.
She is a recipient of the Queen's Platinum Jubilee Medal
and the Edmonton Artists' Trust Fund. She is currently
finishing her master of fine arts in creative writing at
the University of British Columbia, where she is writing
a graphic novel and children's books.
nishapatel.ca